2 KINGS &
2 CHRONICLES
A SELF-STUDY GUIDE

Irving L. Jensen

MOODY PRESS
CHICAGO

Cover photo: The entrance to Samaria

ISBN: 0-8024-4485-7

3 5 7 9 10 8 6 4

Printed in the United States of America

Contents

Introduction

This manual on 2 Kings continues the studies that were begun in 1 Kings. A thorough study of 1 Kings is the best preparation for work on 2 Kings.

Perhaps the most difficult aspect of the study of these history books is the multitude of historical facts involved, including unfamiliar names of the many kings. One of the purposes of this manual is to help you sort out the items of lesser importance, in order to concentrate your attention on the bigger items. It is highly recommended that you use a commentary (*The Wycliffe Bible Commentary* is excellent) especially for help in the historical facts of these books. Also be sure to keep the *Chart of Kings and Prophets* always before you as you study, so that you can place each king and prophet in the appropriate setting as you proceed.

The major purpose of this manual is to help you study these books of the Bible *mainly on your own.* In the study books of this series, various methods of study have been suggested, involving how to *see* what the Bible text says and then how to *record* what is seen. By diligently following the instructions given in each lesson, you will be developing fruitful habits of Bible study.

The frequent use of charts in this and the other books of this series emphasizes the importance of the "eye-gate" in Bible study. Some charts are given in full, for information. Most of the charts are only partially completed; your writing down observations on these charts should open up many doors of new insights into the wonderful Book of God.

Before beginning your study of Lesson 1, become acquainted with the geography maps (pp. 6, 8) and the charts included at the end of this manual. Familiarity with the names of people and places of 2 Kings and 2 Chronicles will greatly aid your study.

Suggestions to Leaders of Classes:

1. If any lesson seems too long for one meeting, take half the assigned work and leave the other half for the next meeting. Undertake no more than the class can do thoroughly.

2. Enlarged copies of the maps and of some of the charts would be of help to the class leader.

3. Insist that members of the class study the lesson at home and bring to the class written answers to the printed questions as far as possible.

4. Urge members of the class to read the assigned chapters in the Bible before they read the comments on them.

5. At the beginning of each meeting have a short review of the previous work.

6. Insist that the members of the class think and study for themselves. Give them opportunities to express their thoughts and tell the lessons they have learned. Refuse to simply lecture.

7. Constantly emphasize the importance of carefully looking up all Scripture references given in each lesson. This should not be neglected.

Lesson 1
General Introduction and Survey

The book of 2 Kings continues the narrative of the history of Israel and Judah where 1 Kings left it.[1] The narratives of both books proceed in a downward trend.

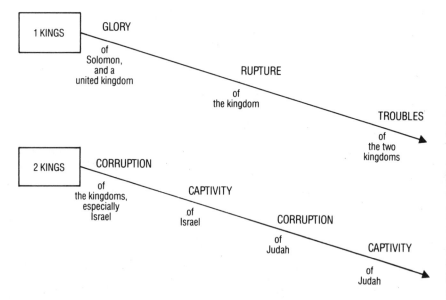

For maximum profit from your study of 2 Kings, you should first study 1 Kings. Since most of the introductory and background

1. In the original Hebrew Bible, 1 and 2 Kings were one book. When the Septuagint translators translated this one book into Greek, they made two books out of it. The reason was that of convenience of handling, since the Greek translation requires about one-third more space than the Hebrew text. This twofold division first appeared in modern Hebrew Bibles with the printed edition of Daniel Bomberg in 1517.

2 KINGS KINGDOMS TAKEN CAPTIVE

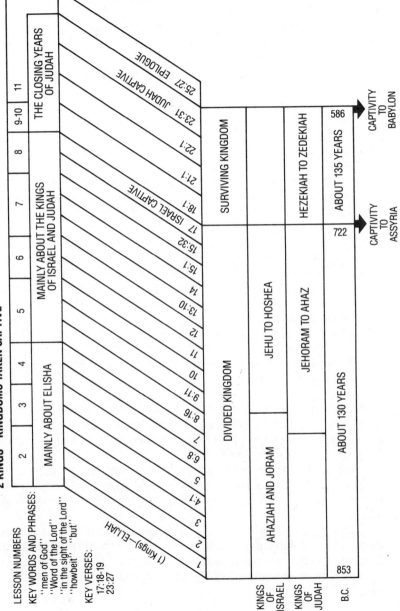

LESSON NUMBERS	2	3	4	5	6	7	8	9-10	11		
	MAINLY ABOUT ELISHA			MAINLY ABOUT THE KINGS OF ISRAEL AND JUDAH				THE CLOSING YEARS OF JUDAH		

KEY WORDS AND PHRASES:
"men of God"
"Word of the Lord"
"in the sight of the Lord"
"howbeit" "but"

KEY VERSES:
17:18-19
23:27

(1 Kings)—ELIJAH

1 2 3 4:1 5 6:8 7 8:16 9:11 10 11 12 13:10 14 15:1 15:32 17 18:1 21:1 22:1 23:31 25:27 EPILOGUE

ISRAEL CAPTIVE JUDAH CAPTIVE

DIVIDED KINGDOM — SURVIVING KINGDOM

KINGS OF ISRAEL: AHAZIAH AND JORAM | JEHU TO HOSHEA

KINGS OF JUDAH: JEHORAM TO AHAZ | HEZEKIAH TO ZEDEKIAH

B.C. 853 | ABOUT 130 YEARS | 722 CAPTIVITY TO ASSYRIA | ABOUT 135 YEARS | 586 CAPTIVITY TO BABYLON

7

material is common to both books, a discussion of these subjects is not given here. Refer to the study manual on 1 Kings for this.

Following the same procedure of the manual of 1 Kings and 1 Chronicles, the present study stays mainly with the narrative of 2 Kings, with supplementary reference to the parallel and unique passages of 2 Chronicles as they have important bearing on the text being studied. (As pointed out in the manual on 1 Kings, the books of 1 and 2 Chronicles record almost exclusively that which has reference to the Davidic line and the southern kingdom of Judah.)

Survey of 2 Kings

The starting place for your study of 2 Kings is a sweeping view of the book as a whole. To accomplish this, scan the entire book in one sitting, if possible, not tarrying over any details. Record a title for each chapter on the accompanying chart. (Note: In some instances one title is to be given for a group of chapters or for part of a chapter.)

What are your first impressions after making this survey? Did you catch any important key words or phrases? If not, be on the lookout for these as you proceed from lesson to lesson, when such words and phrases will stand out more clearly. The identification of key words and phrases in a book is often the best clue to the theme of the book.

Did you notice any turning point in the book? Any climax? Compare the beginning and ending of the book.

Now study the accompanying chart more carefully, noting the following observations:

1. The two main divisions of the book are marked by a heavy line between chapters 17 and 18, the first division being *The Divided Kingdom*, chapters 1-17, and the second division being *The Surviving Kingdom*, chapters 18-25.

We shall find in our study of 2 Kings that up to the end of chapter 17 the two kingdoms, Israel and Judah, are both under consideration as they have been since 1 Kings 12. (See chart on p. 112)

In 2 Kings 17, however, the kingdom of Israel ceased to exist. Because of idolatry the people were taken out of their land into captivity by the Assyrians. And from 2 Kings 18 to the end of the book we have the record of the closing years of the kingdom of Judah.

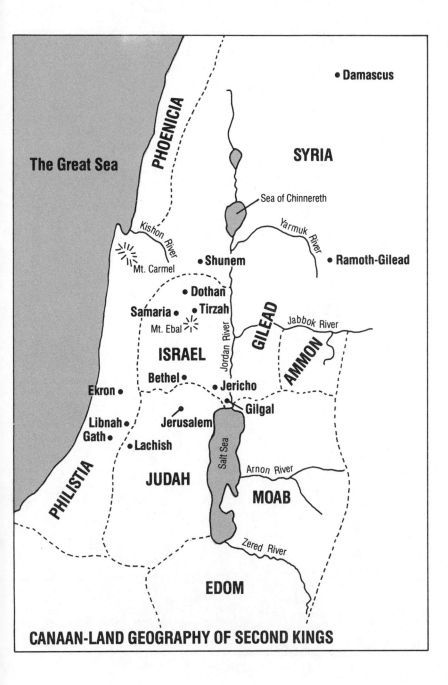

The Great Sea

Damascus

PHOENICIA

SYRIA

Sea of Chinnereth

Kishon River

Mt. Carmel

Yarmuk River

Shunem

Ramoth-Gilead

Dothan

Samaria • Tirzah

Mt. Ebal

Jordan River

GILEAD

Jabbok River

ISRAEL

AMMON

Bethel •

Jericho

Ekron •

Gilgal

Libnah •

Jerusalem

Salt Sea

Gath •

Lachish

Arnon River

PHILISTIA

JUDAH

MOAB

Zered River

EDOM

CANAAN-LAND GEOGRAPHY OF SECOND KINGS

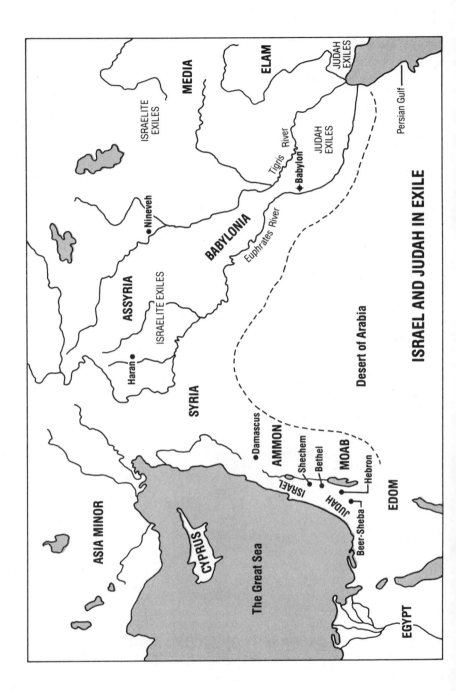

ISRAEL AND JUDAH IN EXILE

2. The book of 2 Kings covers a period of about 265 years. The first division, chapters 1-17, covers about 130 years, whereas the second division, chapters 18-25, covers about 135 years.

3. Observe which chapters record the two critical events of the judgments of Israel and Judah.

4. Note which chapters are devoted to the ministry of Elisha. Observe also that the last of Elijah's ministry is the subject of the opening chapter of the book.

5. The large proportion of space devoted to the ministries of Elijah and Elisha suggests the importance of these men during this era of God's people. The time period covered by 2 Kings has been called the great prophet period. Refer to the *Chart of Kings and Prophets* (pp. 110-11) and identify the various prophets who served between 850 B.C. and 586 B.C.

6. Note from the survey chart the arrangement of 2 Kings's record of the reign of the kings of Israel and Judah.

7. Some key verses and words suggested for this book are shown on the chart. Be on the lookout for others as you proceed with your personal study.

8. The title given to 2 Kings is Kingdoms Taken Captive. The title given to 1 Kings was A Kingdom Divided Against Itself.

9. Since 2 Kings completes the narrative begun in 1 Kings, it will be of interest to compare the beginning of 1 Kings with the end of 2 Kings. Refer to the chart of 1 Kings shown in the study manual for that book, and notice especially such contrasts as:

(a) 1 Kings begins with a kingdom established in glory; 2 Kings ends with a kingdom dissolved in shame.

(b) 1 Kings begins with bright prospects for obedience; 2 Kings ends with tragic judgments for disobedience.

(c) 1 Kings begins with the dazzling splendor of the Temple; 2 Kings ends with the smoke and flames of the Temple in ruins.

10. In your study thus far you have seen some of the prominent points of the book of 2 Kings. Write out a list of some important spiritual lessons that are taught by these.

Prepare to Analyze

Your survey study has been of a cursory nature, since you were not looking primarily for a host of details. Now as you begin to analyze each of the smaller parts of the book, your study procedure will be more exact and comprehensive. But, as you analyze, be sure to keep in the back of your mind the broad movements of 2 Kings. This will help you to analyze more accurately and fully, and it will also prevent your becoming bogged down in the many details of the book.

Remember also the ultimate purpose in studying much of Old Testament history. It is to find the timeless universal *principle* behind the local temporal *detail* of that day so that you may apply the spiritual truths to your own life. Recall 1 Corinthians 10:11, which can be applied to such Bible history: "All these things happened to them as examples, as object lessons to us, to warn us against doing the same things; they were written down so that we could read about them and learn from them in these last days as the world nears its end" (*The Living Bible* [*TLB*]).

What tools are you using for study? You should have at least the following:
1. A good Bible (large print; wide margins; paper conducive to marking)
2. Pens and pencils (various colors)
3. Paper for recording your observations
You will also value the outside help of a good Bible dictionary and a commentary. (*The New Unger's Bible Dictionary* and *The Wycliffe Bible Commentary* are recomended.) Use the commentary for two kinds of help: (1) for explanation of difficult portions of the text during the course of your study; and (2) as a supplement to your own observations after you have completed your independent study.

As you study 2 Kings, put a determined will behind the eye. The Bible—every part of it—is the Book of God. Desire to know what it says and to obey its commands.

Lesson 2

2 Kings 1:1–3:27

Men of God and Enemies of God

A picture of contrasts that shows fearless faithful prophets of God standing firm in the face of defiance by the enemies of God is painted in these chapters. They are colorful for their action, and anyone who reads them must be impressed by the persistence of unbelief and disobedience in the hearts of men who heard God's word by way of the prophets.

I. ANALYSIS

It is important for you, at the outset of your study of 2 Kings, to establish in your mind the setting and continuity of these first chapters of 2 Kings in relation to 1 Kings. To help you do this, read the passages cited below before you read 2 Kings 1:1–3:27.
Read 1 Kings 21:17-29. This passage is the last reference to Elijah in 1 Kings. It has to do with his relations to Ahab.

How was Ahab related to Ahaziah of 2 Kings 1?

_____

_____

Read 1 Kings 22:51-53. This is the last paragraph of 1 Kings. How does it serve as a setting for the first chapters of 2 Kings?

_____

_____

Read 1 Kings 19:19-21. This passage describes Elijah momentarily placing his mantle on Elisha in *anticipation* of the day when Elisha would succeed him in the prophetic office, which takes place in the story of this lesson. There were many prophets during the

MEN OF GOD AND ENEMIES OF GOD
2 KINGS 1:1—3:27

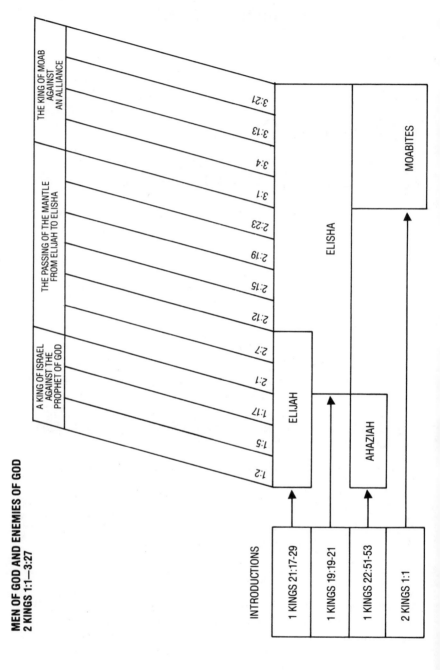

days of Elijah (cf. 2 Kings 2:1-6). How did Elijah know that it was Elisha on whom he was to place his mantle?

_____

_____

After you have gained this acquaintance with the setting of these first chapters of 2 Kings, read through the chapters in one sitting. Try to visualize the action and be sure you know the geographical locations of such places as Samaria, Ekron, Bethel, Jericho, Gilgal, Mount Carmel, Moab, and Edom (see map).

What are your first impressions of this passage?

_____

_____

_____

Record some key words and phrases that stood out in your reading.

_____

_____

Read the passage a second time, and as you proceed from paragraph to paragraph, record paragraph titles on the accompanying chart. Notice from the accompanying chart how this passage is organized. You may want to add to the chart some other outlines of groups of paragraphs.
1. *Chapter 1* (v. 1 is an introduction to 3:4ff.). Who are the main characters of this chapter?

_____

Compare the two.

_____

_____

Baal-zebub (v. 2) is the equivalent of the New Testament Beelzebub. Read Matthew 10:25; 12:24. What marks of a true prophet of God are seen in Elijah in this chapter?

_____

_____

2. *Chapter 2*. Statements made by Elisha in this chapter are of particular interest. For each of the following statements, identify what Elisha meant and why he said what he did:

2:2 "I will not leave thee."

_____

2:3 "Hold ye your peace."

_____

2:9 "Let a double portion of thy spirit be upon me."

_____

2:12 "My father, my father, the chariot of Israel, and the horsemen thereof."

_____

2:14 "Where is the Lord God of Elijah?"

_____

2:16 "Ye shall not send."

_____

2:17 "Send."

_____

2:20 "Put salt therein." (Note: Translate "naught" in v. 19 as "bad.")

_____

2:24 "He . . . cursed them in the name of the Lord."

_____

What different kinds of miracles are recorded in this chapter?

_____

_____

What was God's purpose in giving His prophets such powers?

_____

3. The name *Elijah* appears often in the later books of the Bible. John the Baptist is the New Testament Elijah. Read Malachi 4:5-6; Matthew 11:14; 17:10-13; Mark 9:13; Luke 1:17; John 1:21, 25. Some thought Jesus was a reincarnated Elijah (Matt. 16:13; Mark 6:15; 8:28; Luke 9:8, 19). Read these other references to Elijah in their different settings:

    (a) Mount of Transfiguration (Matt. 17:3-4; Mark 9:4-5; Luke 9:30-33)

    (b) Jesus on the cross (Matt. 27:47, 49; Mark 15:35-36)

    (c) Example of a prevailing prayer (James 5:17-18)

4. Notice the different references to "sons of the prophets." There were obviously many prophets serving in the days of Elijah and Elisha; some were still being trained in the schools of the prophets. Were their services less important to God than those of Elijah and Elisha?

_____

How does God measure service?

_____

5. *Chapter 3.* What do you learn from this chapter about evil alliances, God's sovereign ways, and judgment?

_____

_____

Read verse 27*b* thus: "And there was great indignation in Israel. ..." Cite the ways in which verse 27 is a pungent commentary on life in the days of Elisha.

_____

_____

6. Before you read the Comments section, think back over the three chapters and list some of the vital truths they teach.

_____

_____

_____

_____

II. COMMENTS

A. Israel's King—Ahaziah (1:1-18)

Ahaziah, the eighth king of the ten-tribe kingdom, Israel, was Ahab's oldest son, a very wicked man who reigned less than two years (1 Kings 22:51-53). In the closing days of his life he ignored the presence of God, defied His power, and went to his death unrepentant, as far as the record informs us.

Ahaziah was in the royal palace at Samaria when the accident occurred that made him sick. Fearing that his injuries might prove fatal he sent messengers to Ekron, one of the principal cities of the Philistines not far distant from Samaria, to inquire of Baal-zebub, the god of Ekron, whether or not he would recover. Baal-zebub ("Baal of the fly"; or Baal-zebul, "Baal of the dwelling") was the name under which the god Baal was worshipped at Ekron. This son of Ahab and Jezebel followed the example of his parents in his adherence to false gods.

Ahaziah's action in sending to Baal-zebub was a deliberate rejection of Jehovah and the willful disregard of His presence and power. This same sin had brought the wrath of God on his father's house, and now he too received a message of judgment from the God whom he had insulted.

From the fact that the messengers obeyed Elijah and returned to the king without going to Ekron, it would appear that they must have been convinced that the prophet spoke with divine authority.

When Ahaziah heard the description of the man whom the messengers had met, he immediately recognized him as Elijah, whom no doubt he had seen years before when his father was king. Unimpressed by this message from Jehovah and filled with rage, Ahaziah determined to make Elijah submit to him. A captain, accompanied by his fifty men, was sent to arrest Elijah, but when in the name of the king he insolently commanded the prophet to come down from the top of the hill on which he was sitting, he and his company were instantly consumed by fire, as were also the second captain and his fifty men whom Ahaziah sent.

From Elijah's answer to these two captains we may conclude that they had been grossly disrespectful in addressing him as the prophet of God. F. B. Meyer says, "Either they did not hold him to be a prophet, or they gloried in putting the power of their master above that of Jehovah. In any case the insult was less against Elijah than against Elijah's God." Again God had shown Himself to be the God who answers by fire.

The third captain and his fifty men were spared the judgment that fell upon the other companies, because their attitude toward

18

God and His servant was entirely different. Elijah went with them to the king and delivered in person the message of death that he had sent at the first.

Ahaziah died, and, because he had no son to succeed him, his brother Joram (or Jehoram) took the throne of Israel.

B. The Translation of Elijah (2:1-25)

In chapter 2 of 2 Kings is pictured one of the most sublime scenes in the Old Testament. Some of the highlights of this chapter are:

1. Note that the fact of his translation was known to Elijah, Elisha, and to the sons of the prophets (vv. 5-9). All being prophets, this fact may have been revealed to each of them directly by God. Or Elijah may have transmitted the message to the others.

2. Perhaps Elijah's repeated request of Elisha that he remain at Gilgal and Bethel and Jericho was to test his faithfulness and earnestness, inasmuch as Elisha was to succeed him.

3. The schools of the prophets, probably first established by Samuel (1 Sam. 10:5-10; 19:19-22), were institutions for the instruction and training of the prophets, perhaps something like our theological seminaries and Bible schools. There were such institutions in various places, such as Bethel, Gilgal, and Jericho. The pupils of the older prophets were called "sons of the prophets" (2 Kings 2:3, 5, 7). Elisha, because of the special way in which he was appointed (1 Kings 19:16-19), and because of his close association with Elijah, was acknowledged to be Elijah's successor, and the sons of the prophets were prepared to accept him as their leader in Elijah's place. It is interesting to note that the schools of the prophets were in Israel, not in Judah.

4. The miracle of the divided waters of the river Jordan reminds us of the time that Joshua and the children of Israel walked through the Jordan on dry ground and also of the parted waters of the Red Sea when Moses led the children of Israel out of Egypt.

5. In asking for a "double portion," Elisha was not asking for twice as much of the Spirit as Elijah had. The "double portion" was the portion of the firstborn son. (See Deut. 21:17.) He wanted to be regarded nearest to Elijah's heart, even as a firstborn son. In 2 Kings 2:12 Elisha addressed Elijah as his father. He realized that if he was to carry on Elijah's work he must have Elijah's power, so he asked to be equipped for this service by God.

6. Elijah's experience of verse 11 is unique. Although there are many details one would like to know, we have just this brief statement of the bare facts of this marvelous event. How appropriate that Elijah should be taken from earth in a chariot of fire, since he was the prophet of fire who had called down fire once on

Mount Carmel and twice to consume the enemies of God. It was also appropriate that he who during his ministry had appeared suddenly time and again like a whirlwind should have been swept up to heaven in a whirlwind.

7. Now that Elisha was to take Elijah's place in the prophetic ministry and as the head of the schools of the prophets, he was given (1) the mantle of Elijah, (2) the power of Elijah, and (3) the acknowledgment from the sons of the prophets that he stood in Elijah's room.

8. The sons of the prophets, not having witnessed Elijah's translation, were slow to believe that he had really gone into heaven. They felt confident that his body could be found and were not satisfied until they had made a three-day search. The human heart is not prepared to accept the miraculous.

9. Not only did Elisha have to be acknowledged as Elijah's successor by the schools of the prophets but also by the people of the land. Especially to the enemies of God it had to be demonstrated that he spoke by the Spirit and power of Jehovah. Hence the miracle of healing the waters at Jericho and the punishment of the rash and sacrilegious young men of Bethel. (Note: The Hebrew translated as "little children" in the King James Version really means "young men" and refers to youth who were old enough to understand the wickedness of their conduct.) The young men were, in effect, telling Elisha to leave their presence permanently: "go up" to heaven, just as Elijah "went up" (v. 11) to heaven. The epithet "thou bald head" suggests that they were classifying Elisha as a defiled, disgraceful outcast, for baldness and a shaven head signified leprosy (cf. Isa. 3:17). They did not want prophets of God around to hamper their loose sinful living. These young men were children of the Baal worshipers and course had been taught contempt for the true worshipers of God. Thus their insult was aimed not only at Elisha but also at God. Therefore, the judgment that so suddenly overtook them was not primarily to avenge Elisha but to vindicate Jehovah's honor.

Passing from Bethel, Elisha went on to Mount Carmel, the spot ever associated with the name of Elijah. The purpose of this visit is not mentioned, but one can easily surmise that at the outset of his career Elisha wished to retire for a while to be alone with God, to look out over his field of labor, face its difficulties, and gird his spirit for the conflict. And what more fitting place could he have chosen than this mountain where God had so wondrously manifested His presence and power; where Elijah had, in the power of the Spirit, stood alone against the 450 prophets of Baal, challenging them to prove the claims of their god; where the prayer of the prophet had opened heaven and brought down fire and flood.

Elisha's heart must have been stirred as he thought of these things about which no doubt he and Elijah had often talked. How he must have been encouraged to believe that as God had been with Elijah so He would be with him. Descending the mountain, Elisha went to Samaria, the city that became his permanent residence for many years (2 Kings 2:25). From this place he seems to have made circuits in every direction over the whole country, instructing the people at large.

C. Alliance vs. Moab (3:1-27)

The iniquitous reign of Ahab's son Ahaziah lasted less than two years. Since he had no sons, he was succeeded on the throne of Israel by his brother Joram, who, though not as bad as his father or his mother, was nevertheless a wicked man.

Moab, which had been subject to Israel and had been paying enormous annual taxes, rebelled and was threatening to become troublesome. King Joram apparently considered his own army insufficient to subdue the revolting Moabites; therefore he sent a request to King Jehoshaphat of Judah to join him in this war.

As shown by 2 Chronicles 20, Jehoshaphat had already won an overwhelming victory over the Moabites and the Ammonites when they invaded his land, and Joram no doubt hoped that with Jehoshaphat as his ally there would be similar success in the present venture. Of Jehoshaphat's willingness to join him he evidently felt sure, remembering the alliances Jehoshaphat had made with both his father, Ahab, and his brother Ahaziah when they were reigning.

As expected, Jehoshaphat readily gave his consent to the proposition, and the king of Edom also joined his forces. So these three kings made their plans for the campaign against Moab. It was agreed that instead of crossing the Jordan and entering Moab from the north, they would march through the land of Judah down to the southern end of the Dead Sea, going through the wilderness of Edom, and attack Moab from the southwest. (Follow the journey on a map.)

After a seven-day march the three confederate kings discovered upon reaching the border of Moab that there was no water for man or beast. Notice in this crisis the difference in the attitude of Joram, the wicked king of Israel, and that of Jehoshaphat, the good king of Judah (2 Kings 3:11-13). Jehoram *blamed* God; Jehoshaphat *sought* God.

We are not told how the prophet Elisha happened to be with the army at this time, but from his words to the three kings who came to seek his counsel we see that he, like Elijah, was absolutely fearless and uncompromising (2 Kings 3:13-15).The king of Moab in desperation sacrificed his eldest son, heir to his throne, to conciliate his god, Chemosh (2 Kings 3:26-27). The Israelites were indignant over such an abominable act, but this was apparently as far as their reaction went, for the text concludes, "And they departed from him, and returned to their own land." And, it might be added, to their own abominable ways.

III. SUMMARY

Each of these three chapters of 2 Kings tells something of the sovereign ways of God with His chosen people, the seed of Abraham.

Chapter 1: God judges a king of His people.

Chapter 2: God speaks to His people by prophets.

Chapter 3: God delivers His people from an enemy.

When we look at all three parts of this story and remember that God had thus dealt with His people on various other occasions before this, we cannot help but see anew what a long-suffering and merciful God our Jehovah is.

Miracles of Elisha

The successor of Elijah, the prophet Elisha, is the key figure of 2 Kings, even as Elijah was the central figure of 1 Kings. In our present lesson we shall be almost wholly occupied with Elisha. Interesting comparisons may be made of these two representatives of God. Elijah is noted for great public acts, whereas Elisha is distinguished by the large number of miracles he performed, many of them for individual needs. Elijah's ministry emphasized God's law, judgment, and severity. Elisha supplemented this by demonstrating God's grace, love, and tenderness. Elijah was like John the Baptist, thundering the message of repentance for sin. Elisha followed this up by going about, as Christ did, doing deeds of kindness and by performing miracles attesting that the words of the prophets were from God.

In chapter 4 are recorded five miracles, all of which emphasize the power and goodness of Jehovah. Each one is calculated to testify to the presence of God in Israel and His willingness to do for the whole nation what was done for the individuals who benefited by the miracles. If only the nation would turn to Him in faith as these individuals turned to Elisha, His representative!

We must not lose sight of the religious situation in the northern kingdom of Israel at that time. Never since the kingdom was formed under Jeroboam had the people of these ten tribes availed themselves of the Temple worship at Jerusalem. Neither had they had the ministry of the priests and Levites, because the priests and Levites, together with many devout worshipers of God, had fled into Judah under the persecution of Jeroboam. (See 2 Chron. 11:13-16.)

However the schools of the "sons of the prophets" were evidently a power for righteousness in Israel. These schools of the prophets were colleges for instruction in the law of God, and no doubt the prophets taught the people what they themselves had learned. A prophet is a spokesman for God, not only a *foreteller* of future events but also a *forth-teller* of the truth. These prophets performed somewhat the same services for the northern kingdom that the priests did for the southern kingdom.

Elisha was the acknowledged head of the prophetic body, and he journeyed up and down the land making frequent visits to each of these schools. It was while he was engaged in these duties that many of his miracles were performed. In fact, one of his miracles was performed for the benefit of one of the sons of the prophets (the last miracle of this lesson).

I. ANALYSIS

First read 4:1–6:7 in one sitting, making notations in your Bible as you read. What impressed you most about these stories?
By filling out the accompanying work sheet you will be able to see something of the overall ministry of Elisha.

1. *See 4:1-7.* Does it appear from this account that the widow may have been a believer?

_____

When did the oil of the widow's pot cease to flow?

_____

What spiritual truth does this illustrate?

_____

2. *See 4:8-17.* Why is hospitality an important Christian grace?

_____

What does this story teach about the principle of *rewards?*

_____

Can you recall any words of Christ in which He promised rewards for hospitality?

_____

_____

3. *See 4:18-37.* Try to feel the emotions of the mother in these experiences. Why did she answer, "It is well," to Gehazi?

_____

24

2 KINGS 4:1—6:7

PASSAGE	PERSONS INVOLVED IN THE MIRACLES	PROBLEMS BRINGING ON THE MIRACLES	DESCRIPTIONS OF THE MIRACLES	SIGNIFICANCE OF, AND SPIRITUAL TRUTHS TAUGHT BY, THE MIRACLES
4:1-7				
4:8-17				
4:18-37				
4:38-41				
4:42-44				
5:1-19				
5:20-27				
6:1-7				

What does verse 31a teach?

_____

_____

4. *See 4:38-41.* What is the miracle of verse 41?

_____

_____

Compare this story with that of the addition of salt to the waters in 2:19-22.

    salt + bad waters = good waters
    meal + poisoned food = good food

Apply these illustrations to today as to God's using "salt" and "bread" to do His work.

_____

_____

5. *See 4:42-44.* Of what New Testament story does this remind you?

_____

_____

6. *See 5:1-19.* The healing of Naaman, head of the Syrian army, was the highlight of Elisha's ministry of miracles. The story is a classic illustration of the spiritual truths about the salvation of a soul. Reread each item of the narrative, noting the facts that illustrate such truths as:

    (a) lost condition of man
    (b) God's witnesses of this gospel
    (c) man's main search for salvation
    (d) God's invitation to salvation
    (e) obstacles to salvation
    (f) the true way of salvation
    (g) results of salvation

7. *See 5:20-27.* What was the sin here, and how did the judgment match the sin?

_____

_____

8. *See 6:1-7.* Some have suggested that this school of the prophets was located at Jericho. What is implied by the reference of 6:1 that the prophets' dwelling was too small for them?

_____

What is suggested by the request of one of the prophets that Elisha go along?

In terms of the miracle, what is the significance of the fact that the ax head had been borrowed?

---

9. Review the stories of this section and list some of the truths God was trying to teach the people through these events.

II. COMMENTS

A. The Increase of the Widow's Oil (4:1-7)

This widow had lost her husband and her money and was about to lose her sons, but she had not lost her faith in God. She went to God's prophet, confessing her poverty, her helplessness, and her distress. Her unquestioning obedience to Elisha's instructions proves the sincerity of her faith. How abundantly God supplied her every need, as He will always do for anyone who comes to Him in humility and faith and willingness to obey. He would have done the same for Israel if they had turned to Him.

It should be noted that in Israel a child could be sold into servitude for debt (cf. Ex. 21:7; Deut. 15:12-18; Lev. 25:9-34; Jer. 34:8-16).

B. The Shunammite Woman Given a Son (4:8-17)

This woman entertained the prophet Elisha whenever he passed through Shunem. She was called a "great woman." The word "great" is sometimes used in the Old Testament to suggest wealth or influence, as in 1 Samuel 25:2 and 2 Samuel 18:32. We gather from the narrative that this Shunammite's home was one of affluence and that she was a woman whose keen perception and decisive character would make her influential.

In these verses the woman is seen to be great in other ways also. She was great in her interest in the work of God. She did what she did for Elisha because she perceived that he was one of God's servants doing God's work.

She was great in her contentment. When Elisha, wishing to reward her in some way for all her thoughtfulness, care, and expenditure for his comfort, offered to use his influence with the king or the military commander, she quietly replied, "I dwell among mine own people." No doubt Elisha, after all he had done for the king and the army, as recorded in chapter 3, could have asked and received great favor for this woman and her husband; but she had no desire for worldly advancement such as the king could give her. She was content with her home, her position, and her friends.

But Elisha knew, when Gehazi told him that she was childless, what he would ask God to do for her. To be childless was to a Hebrew woman a great grief. When Elisha told her she was to have a son within the year, the news seemed too good to be true. She begged him not to raise hopes that could not be realized. But Elisha was speaking for God, who was able to perform such a promise. In due time she gave birth to a son.

C. The Shunammite's Son Restored to Life (4:18-37)

Again, this woman was great in her faith. When her child was stricken, her self-restraint and quiet faith under the shock of her great calamity were remarkable. If God could give her a child, then He could give it back to her, she reasoned. Without a moment's hesitation she laid the child on the prophet's bed and hastened, as fast as her servant could drive, to Mount Carmel, a distance of about fifteen miles.

Her answer ("It is well") to Elisha's servant was made with no thought to deceive. The phrase of the King James Version translates a Hebrew word meaning "peace." By answering thus she was putting aside further questioning until she reached Elisha, and she was also saying that all would come out all right.

The woman was not insensitive to the grief of knowing her son had died. She would speak of her grief to no one but to the "man of God." And when she finally came to him, she wanted to know the prophet's explanation of this tragic turn of events. The prophet was the sponsor of the gift of the child in the first place —she had not asked for a child. Now the child was dead. Was Elisha aware of another piece in the pattern, which he had not disclosed to her? The text does not reveal any answer by Elisha. His answer was to act, and before long the dead son was alive again.

Elisha's rod in the hands of Gehazi had no effect upon the dead child, and from what we learn of Gehazi a little later it is not surprising that God did not work miracles through him.

Notice that before the rejoicing mother clasped to her heart her restored child, she bowed in thanksgiving for the wondrous favor that God had granted.

D. The Noxious Pottage Purified (4:38-41)

In these verses we see Elisha in one of the schools of the prophets. We can well imagine how he would be welcomed by those students at Gilgal—how they would sit around him as he instructed them and told them of his experiences. Perhaps he related to them how God had magnified His power in the increase of the widow's oil and in raising the Shunammite's son. And now they too were privileged to see an exhibition of the power of God. There was "death in the pot," but God had power over death, and they were saved when they cried to Elisha.

Notice that each miracle was the result of a direct turning to Elisha, and Elisha stood for Jehovah in the land. Elisha was God's representative, a "man of God."

E. One Hundred Men Miraculously Fed (4:42-44)

If this paragraph is dated at the time of the preceding one, then it was a time of famine in the land. Whatever the case, this gift of food, although greatly appreciated, was insufficient for one hundred men, except as God made the supply adequate. This miracle foreshadows the miracles of our Lord in feeding the multitudes (Matt. 14:19-21; 15:32-39).

F. The Healing of Naaman (5:1-19)

The miracle of Naaman's healing is one of the finest pictures in the entire Bible of the healing of the sinner. It also is one of the many Old Testament stories that present the way of salvation with plainness. Note the several points of correspondence:

1. *The Sinner Before He Comes to God* (5:1)
Much could be said in Naaman's favor. He was great, successful, wealthy, honorable, mighty in the eyes of his master and of men, *"but he was a leper."* He had a loathsome, incurable disease that was eating away his life. Fortunately for him, he knew and realized his condition. To escape from this living death was his great concern.

29

Many today are perishing from the loathsome leprosy of sin. One may be great, successful, wealthy, honorable, and mighty, but spiritually lost. To realize one's lost condition before God and to desire to escape from it are the first steps toward salvation. Naaman discovered this.

2. *God's Messengers of the Gospel* (5:2-3)

God's messenger in this case was a little captive slave girl. She was humble, weak, and insignificant—as are many of God's messengers—but she knew the one all-essential thing: that with God there is healing. And she knew how to lead others to be cured.

God's faithful witnesses are not afraid or ashamed to testify of their God and to tell others that with Him there is healing for any and for all.

3. *Where Salvation Cannot Be Found* (5:4-7)

These verses give a true pattern of the disposition of human nature: looking first to human sources for help and trusting in power, position, and riches. When Naaman went (read 4*a* as "and he went in") to his master, the king of Syria, and told him what the maid had said, the king consented to send a request for help, but he would only think of seeking help from the *king* of Israel, not a *prophet* of God. Further, the king of Syria thought that help would come only if it was bought, so he sent costly gifts with Naaman for the king. Naaman was carried along by the thinking of his master, the king, and he, like the king, had to learn that the gifts of God cannot be purchased. They are simply to be received—a hard lesson for the human heart.

Verse 7 shows how all Naaman's hopes of receiving help from human sources had to be shattered before he would turn to the true source.

(Note: The king of Israel is not identified by name in this story. We cannot be sure which one it was, since the *chronological* locations of the Elisha stories of this section are omitted from the author's narrative because he was more interested in 'a *topical* arrangement.)

4. *God Doesn't Close the Door to a Seeking Soul* (5:8)

This verse is a good illustration of the way in which God watches over the seeking soul and speaks just at the moment when all other means of help have failed. When Elisha heard about the king's violent reaction to Naaman's appeal, he asked the king to refer Naaman to him. Elisha, as God's representative, said, "Let him come now to me"—the words that God would speak to every anxious soul. In God, and in God alone, there is hope.

5. The Simplicity of the Way of Salvation (5:10)

"Elisha sent a messenger to him, saying, Go and wash in the Jordan seven times, . . . and thou shalt be clean." A simple thing to do, surely; but Naaman objected. He was willing to pay any price, willing to do any great deed of prowess, to make any fatiguing pilgrimage, but he was unwilling to obey a simple command to "wash and be clean." To wash in Jordan's comparatively dirty waters seemed unreasonable and ridiculous to him. But he missed the whole point. The issue was not dirty water or clean water, not reasonableness or unreasonableness; the issue was simply obedience or disobedience. So it is with salvation for the sinner. The sinner must obey God's command to "believe on the Lord Jesus Christ," even though such a way may seem too simple to be real.

6. Pride Has No Place at the Foot of the Cross (5:9, 11-12)

Verse 9 suggests two things about Naaman: (1) he was earnest and sincere, for he came to Elisha for help; (2) he came in pride. It must have been an imposing company with horses and chariots that drew up before Elisha's humble dwelling place. Naaman had come to the right place but not in right spirit. His pride had to be brought low. We see this pride expressing itself in verses 11 and 12.

Conceit is typical of the unregenerate heart. "But Naaman was wroth, and went away, and said, Behold, *I thought* . . ." This leprous, dying man had the presumption to devise in his own mind exactly the plan by which he wanted his cure to be effected. And because God's plan did not correspond with his, he was angry and refused to meet the required conditions. Likewise, men and women today want to be saved in their own way, not in God's way.

Verse 12 shows that in Naaman's heart a struggle was going on between faith on the one hand and unbelief on the other. It was the crucial moment for Naaman, and Satan was trying hard to get the victory, as he does with every person on the point of making the great decision. Satan first appealed to Naaman's *reason*: "See how unreasonable this remedy is. If bathing is the cure for leprosy, there are far better streams than this Jordan in which to wash." He argued, "Are not Abana and Pharpar, rivers of Damascus, better than all the waters of Israel?"

Satan also played on Naaman's *pride* and pointed to the way in which he had been treated. Naaman, a great personage, had come to make a request of a king and pay handsomely for services rendered. First he was sent to the lowly dwelling of a prophet, who did not even come out to meet him, and then he was sent off in this way, without any display or notice, to wash in the muddy

Jordan River. So he turned away in a rage, and it seemed as though Satan had won.

7. *The Value of Persuasion by a Personal Worker* (5:13)
Here we see the value of personal work. The few timely words of advice from Naaman's true friends just at the right moment led him to accept God's way. Often when a soul is in the balance and undecided whether to refuse or obey God, a word will turn the scale one way or the other. Happy is that one who has at hand a friend who will point him in the right direction.

8. *Salvation Is Instantaneous After the Obedience of Faith* (5:14)
The journey from Samaria to the river was a test of Naaman's faith, and the repeated dipping shows that he obeyed absolutely. So Naaman was healed in the same way that every sinner has been saved—through faith and obedience to the Word of God. Notice how instantaneous and thorough the cleansing was—"his flesh came again like unto the flesh of a little child, and he was clean." And not only was his flesh clean and fair as that of a little child, but also his heart had been purified. He was a new creature. From henceforth he would worship and serve the God who had given him life.

9. *Gratitude—A Firstfruit of a Saved Soul* (5:15-17)
These verses show the gratitude and confession of a saved soul. Back to Samaria Naaman hurried, and in the presence of all his company he gave his testimony and rendered thanksgiving to God. This is the first instinct of the regenerate heart. In his gratitude, Naaman urged Elisha to accept the gifts he had brought. But in order that Naaman could fully understand that God's prophet was no greedy heathen priest and that His gifts were free, Elisha took no reward. The only return Naaman could make to God was to lead a life of faith and obedience. This he was only too willing to render, and he asked that he might take back two mules' burden of earth (cf. Ex. 20:24) with which to erect in Damascus an altar to Jehovah for a memorial, or witness, to the God of Israel in his own land. On this he would offer sacrifices, because he declared his determination to forsake all other gods and worship Jehovah alone the rest of his life.

10. *New Christians Must Avoid the Appearance of Evil as They Continue in Their Old Environment* (5:18-19)
As servant of the king of Syria, Naaman knew that his obligations of service would continue. He anticipated being seen bowing in the house of the Syrians' god Rimmon (Hadad), and he did not

want this to be misunderstood as an act of disloyalty to his new Lord.

G. The Sin and Judgment of Gehazi (5:20-27)

The remainder of the chapter tells of Gehazi's covetousness and unworthy conduct, which compromised not only Elisha but the true religion itself. The words "As the Lord liveth" came lightly to his lips, but they meant little to him. Instead of realizing that the Lord did live, and was reading his heart, Gehazi let his thoughts run on, imagining all the garments, olive yards, and vineyards, sheep and oxen, menservants, and maidservants, which his ill-gotten talents would purchase.

Gehazi might well represent those who are engaged in religious work for personal gain, rather than for God's glory. Such persons seek only reward. They desire gold but would rather secure it under the guise of religiosity. Their hearts are set on material possessions. Their condemnation is sure and awful. "The leprosy of Naaman shall cleave to you, and to your descendants for ever" (5:27, *Revised Standard Version* [RSV]), said Elisha, in reply to Gehazi's untruthful statement, "Your servant went nowhere" (5:25, RSV). "And he went out from his presence a leper as white as snow" (5:27).

H. The Lost Ax Head Recovered (6:1-7)

A. C. Gaebelein says regarding this miracle: "There is much comfort for God's trusting children in the miracle of the swimming iron. The mighty power of God condescends to help those who trust [Him] even in the smallest things of life. Our Lord fills the throne in Glory and is the upholder of all things, yet as the sympathizing priest He enters into the lives of His people."[1] There is nothing too great for God to do, and there is nothing too small to ask His aid in doing.

III. SUMMARY

In this lesson we have learned about various needs of people in Elisha's day, and how God, working through Elisha, filled those needs in His abounding grace. As a summary exercise, try to recall the various miracles, the needs they filled, and the spiritual truths they teach.

1. A. C. Gaebelein, *The Annotated Bible, Joshua-Chronicles* (New York: Publication Office "Our Hope," 1915), p. 318

Lesson 4

Elisha's Further Ministries

In this lesson we continue our study of selected events in the ministry of Elisha, who is identified in the Bible as a "man of God."

It is important to recognize that the stories about Elisha, as given in 4:1–8:15, were not intended to follow a consistent chronological sequence. Instead, the author had a topical arrangement in mind, and this is one of the things we should look for in our study. You will note that in this section (4:1–8:15) the kings of Israel who appear in these stories are not identified by name. This makes it difficult for us to date each event, but it also confirms the fact that the author was not emphasizing the time element in the stories.

After this section in 2 Kings, Elisha is placed in the background of the narrative until, in chapter 13, his fatal sickness and death are recorded.

I. ANALYSIS

The way to approach this section is to study it paragraph by paragraph first and then to look for groupings of paragraphs according to common content. The accompanying chart shows paragraph divisions. Mark them in your Bible before reading the section.

Now read 6:8–8:15 in one sitting, being "paragraph conscious" while you read. Record a paragraph title on the chart for each of the twelve paragraphs. Your paragraph titles should be no longer than a few words; choose titles with picture or action words if possible.

Before studying the outlines shown on the accompanying chart, review the entire section with the aid of your paragraph titles, and try to determine how the paragraphs might be grouped together. Then compare your outline with the ones shown.

ELISHA'S FURTHER MINISTRIES
2 KINGS 6:8—8:15

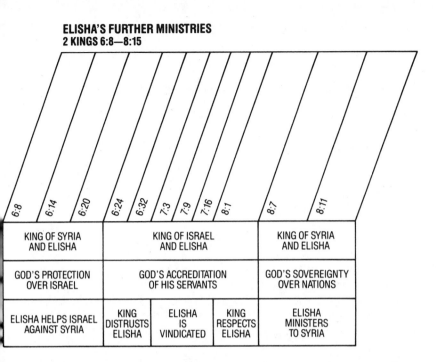

6:8	6:14	6:20	6:24	6:32	7:3 / 7:9 / 7:16 / 8:1	8:7 / 8:11
KING OF SYRIA AND ELISHA			KING OF ISRAEL AND ELISHA			KING OF SYRIA AND ELISHA
GOD'S PROTECTION OVER ISRAEL			GOD'S ACCREDITATION OF HIS SERVANTS			GOD'S SOVEREIGNTY OVER NATIONS
ELISHA HELPS ISRAEL AGAINST SYRIA			KING DISTRUSTS ELISHA	ELISHA IS VINDICATED	KING RESPECTS ELISHA	ELISHA MINISTERS TO SYRIA

1. *See 6:8-13.* What is the miracle of this paragraph?

_____

Compare the setting of this miracle with that of the previous one (6:1-7).

_____

_____

Compare the explanation of the Syrian king (6:11) and that of his servant (6:12).

_____

_____

2. *See 6:14-19.* What did Elisha have in mind when he spoke his words of 6:16?

_____

_____

Contrast the two miracles of 6:17 and 6:18.

_____

Make some spiritual applications from this paragraph.

_____

3. *See 6:20-23*. What was Elisha's strategy here?

_____

Account for the kindnesses of verses 22-23, in view of the raiding band's original mission (6:13-14).

_____

4. *See 6:24-31*. (Though the setting of the story of this and the following paragraphs involves the king of Syria and his siege of the city of Samaria, the main characters are the king of Israel and Elisha—see outline on the chart.) Why did the king of Israel blame Elisha for the abominable situation described in 6:28-29?

_____

Consider a possible answer in 6:20-23.

5. *See 6:32—7:2*. Apparently the king's viewpoint changed in the meantime (cf. 6:33). Account for this.

_____

What were the two prophecies of Elisha, in 7:1 and 7:2?

_____

6. *See 7:3-8*. Contrast the lepers of verse 3 with the same men of verse 8.

_____

Was the miracle of this paragraph primarily for the lepers' benefit?

_____

What does this teach about God's methods of accomplishing His purposes?

_____

7. *See 7:9-15*. Make a contemporary application of the statement "This day is a day of good tidings, and we hold our peace."

_____

_____

8. *See 7:16-20*. Observe the fulfillments of Elisha's two prophecies. Were the fulfillments of more value to Elisha himself or to the people of Israel?

_____

_____

9. *See 8:1-6*. What was the king's estimate of Elisha here?

_____

_____

Contrast this with 6:31.

_____

_____

Note the outline on the accompanying chart.
10. *See 8:7-10*. Account for the Syrian king's respect for Elisha as a "man of God."

_____

_____

Observe how Elisha stood for the truth, even though the message hurt.
11. *See 8:11-15*. Observe the various emotions of this paragraph. What prophecies are here?

_____

Compare 8:13 with 1 Kings 19:15.

_____

_____

Notice the fulfullment of 8:15*b*.
12. Think back over this section and write a list of spiritual lessons taught by this part of God's Scriptures.

_____

_____

_____

_____

II. COMMENTS

A. Elisha Makes Known Ben-hadad's Plans (6:8-12)

Not only God's power but His wisdom is given to His trusting ones. Hostilities with Syria still continued, principally in the form of plundering parties that frequently lay in ambush, ready to spring upon the Israelites sent to repulse them. Again and again, however, these Syrian marauders were foiled through Elisha's God-given insight, until the king of Syria determined to put a stop to the annoyance by capturing the prophet.

B. Elisha and the Syrians (6:13-23)

Throughout this whole narrative, carefully observe Elisha's bearing—calm, peaceful, unruffled, confident. We have here exhibited, for our learning and example, the security of God's servants from both the surprises and the open attacks of the enemy; the confidence and clear vision of one who is in constant communion with God; the peace that he may enjoy when others are distracted by circumstances; and the sure answer to the prayers of a righteous man.

How futile are the attempts to harm those who are under the protection of God. How blessed to be fully assured that God is a very present help in trouble and to be able, as was Elisha, to look past the threatening dangers to the protecting hosts of God, knowing for a surety that "they that be with us are more than they that be with them."

Elisha's words of verse 19 are not an untruth, as "his real residence was Samaria; and in the end he led them to himself, not to harm them, but to repay evil with good (vv. 21-23)."[1]

C. Samaria Under Siege and Famine (6:24–7:20)

The king of Syria was determined, if possible, to conquer the whole territory of the ten tribes. Accordingly, he gathered the entire fighting force of his kingdom and besieged Samaria. The king of Israel was unprepared to meet so strong an army. So, with the leaders of the nation, he shut himself up in Samaria. Although the walls of the city made the people secure from capture, famine soon began to take its toll. Elisha, who was also in the city, kept urging the king and the people to repent of their sins, to call upon

1. James M. Gray, *Christian Workers' Commentary* (New York: Revell, 1915), p. 187.

God, and to trust Him to being about their deliverance. No doubt he rehearsed the many experiences in their history when circumstances had appeared just as hopeless, yet God had delivered them. As far as we know, Elisha was the only man in Samaria who trusted the Lord for deliverance. However, the faith of one man brought the blessing.

The famine soon reached extreme proportions. Actually, the people were reaping judgment for their sins. Moses had foretold that just such hardships and horrors as these would result if the nation refused to keep God's laws. (Cf. Lev. 26:29 and Deut. 28:53-57.) But the king of Israel, instead of pondering the *cause* of these calamities and grieving for the offense, was filled with rage against the prophet.

The prophecy of 2 Kings 7:1 shows that Elisha's eyes were not upon the scarcity in Samaria but upon God's ability to provide, and the next day proved the wisdom of his confidence. Those chariots and horses of fire, invisible to the natural eye but real to the eye of faith, put to flight the formidable enemies while the Israelites slept, and food in abundance was provided.

Once again the living God, in His abundant grace, delivered His people from famine and the sword. It was a narrow escape. They had been allowed to come to that extremity in order that their deliverance might have the highest effect. But so hardened had they become in sin that there was not a sign of repentance or of turning to God in gratitude, either on the part of the king or the people. Could it possibly be that the seven-year famine brought by the Lord as recorded in 8:1 was judgment for the people's refusal to respond to His grace here?

The nation persisted in idolatry and sin, and there was no alternative but the fulfillment of God's word by Moses—that the people should be cast out of their land and scattered abroad. But God was long-suffering, and year after year, generation after generation, we see Him patiently laboring with His people, alternately chastening and blessing, leading and reasoning, ever trying to turn them from their course of folly.

Thus God is dealing today with each rebellious soul. The blessings and the trials, the pleasures and the pain, are but God's attempts to draw the heart away from its idols to Himself.

D. The Shunammite's Land Restored (8:1-6)

The Shunammite's past kindness to God's servant was requited her, first by Elisha's warning of the coming famine and afterward by the restoration of her land.

Except for the knowledge that God is watching every detail of the lives of His own, and making all things work together for good to them that love Him, (Rom. 8:28-29), we should think it a remarkable coincidence that this woman should appear before the king just at the time that Gehazi was rehearsing to him all of Elisha's miracles and just at the moment when mention had been made of the raising of her son from the dead.

E. Elisha, Ben-hadad, Hazael—a Prophet, a King, a Murderer (8:7-15)

In these verses we see Elisha sent to Damascus (locate on map) to be the mouthpiece of God to Syria regarding the change of dynasty that was imminent.

The Old Testament records the history of other nations usually in their relation to God's chosen people. Frequently, as in this case, He used a nation as a rod to chastise Israel.

On the throne of Syria God put Hazael—a man as heartless, cruel, and unscrupulous as he was able and successful.

Although Israel deserved punishment for their departure from God, Elisha's loving heart was pained at the sufferings they were to endure at the hands of Hazael. As he spoke of it to Hazael, the tears flowed down his cheeks. If Elisha was thus grieved, how much more the heart of God. And yet, as a loving mother would permit her child to suffer pain in an endeavor to save its life, so God sent this terrible affliction upon His own people.

We have no detailed account of Hazael's cruelty to Israel, but from 2 Kings 10:32 and 13:3, 22 we have hints that the evils that Elisha mentioned were fully carried out by this new king of Syria.

III. SUMMARY

These stories about Elisha reveal how faithfully and successfully he fulfilled his mission to be a servant of God.

To his own nation he gave all kinds of help to spare it destruction by enemies from without.

To king and people alike he spoke the truth—the word that he received from God—despite the consequences.

To a foreign nation he fulfilled the divine commission to deliver God's message concerning its future, though he was grief-stricken over the terrible judgments upon Israel that were involved.

In all his ways Elisha remained true to God, strong in faith, warm in love, and persevering in tribulation. He was truly a "man of God."

The Beginning of the End of Israel

The "beginning of the end" of Israel concerns the years of the reign of King Jehu, who is the main character of the chapters of this present lesson. The reference is 2 Kings 10:32a, "In those days the Lord *began to cut Israel short.*" Israel, the northern kingdom, had not had a good ruler since its inception, but God in His mercy kept wooing the nation to return to Him in repentance and to acknowledge Him as Lord. This was why He sent them such prophets as Elijah and Elisha. But Israel did not respond. Now in the reign of King Jehu things had come to the point of no return. In Jehu were revived the sins of Jeroboam; Israel forfeited its last chance; eventual doom—captivity—was sure.

At 8:16 the book of 2 Kings picks up the earlier pattern of describing the kingdoms of Israel and Judah alternately, a pattern that appeared first in 1 Kings 12 and continued up to the sections about Elijah and Elisha. Consult the survey chart on page 7 and notice how a new division for 2 Kings is made at 8:16, thus:

1:1	8:16	18:1 25:30
MAINLY ABOUT ELISHA	MAINLY ABOUT THE KINGS OF ISRAEL AND JUDAH	THE CLOSING YEARS OF JUDAH

It would help you also at this point to review the charts *The Setting of Kings and Chronicles* (p. 112) and *Chart of Kings and Prophets* (pp. 110-11), in order to see the setting of the chapters of this lesson. The following excerpt applies to the present lesson (the shaded areas identify the kings of the narrative). Refer to this as you read the text, as a help in distinguishing the kings from each other. Do not let the many references to kings in this book

41

bog you down. (Note: Joram of 8:21-24 is Jehoram of Judah. Mark this in your Bible.)

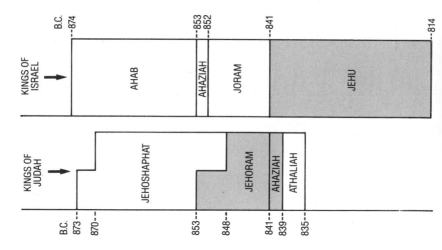

I. ANALYSIS

First read 8:16–10:36 in one sitting. Then return to the text and, following again the method of paragraph-to-paragraph study, record below the main content of each paragraph. Use as few words as possible.

After you have read the 2 Kings passage, read 2 Chronicles for what it adds to this narrative.

1. *See 8:16-19.* What caused a king of *Judah* to walk "in the way of the kings of *Israel*"? (Note the word "for" in v. 18.) Read 1 Kings 16:29-33 and note that Ahab sponsored Baal worship in Israel. In light of the fact that Baal worship was introduced in Judah in Jehoram's reign, measure the long-suffering and mercy of the Lord as shown by 8:19.

_____

_____

_____

2. *See 8:20-24.* Notice the references to Judah's *losses* here. Note also the losses recorded by 2 Chronicles 21:16-17. What spiritual principle is demonstrated here?

_____

2 KINGS 8:16—10:36

KINGDOM	PARAGRAPH	MAIN PERSONS	MAIN ACTIONS	OTHER POINTS
JUDAH	8:16ff.			
	20			
	25			
ISRAEL	9:1			
	11			
	14			
	17			
	27			
	30			
	10:1			
	12			
	15			
	18			
	28			
	32			

Compare your answer with 2 Chronicles 21:12-15.

Note the details of Jehoram's death in 2 Chronicles 21:18-19, and the chronicler's comment of 21:20.

3. *See 8:25-29.* Read 2 Chronicles 22:1-6 in connection with this paragraph. What evil entangling alliance is cited in these verses?

What does the New Testament warn about such relationships?

4. *See 9:1-10.* Harmonize the sovereignty of God in appointing Jehu as king of Israel (vv. 1-6) with the prophecies of verses 7-10.

What is the significance of the fact that as of this time God still referred to Israel as "the people of the Lord"? (9:6).

5. *See 9:11-37.* According to the previous verses (1-10) God appointed Jehu as new king of Israel. Now the story proceeds to show how Jehu disposed of King Joram and others of his circle. Are all the *ways* and *methods* of Jehu's conspiracy necessarily the righteous will of God?

What should be the Christian's view on the saying "The end justifies the means"?

On the slaying of Ahaziah (9:27-28) compare 2 Chronicles 22:7-9.
6. *See 10:1-17.* These paragraphs relate Jehu's slaughters in a bloodthirsty program of wiping out all the males of the house of Ahab. Study the following verses:
- (a) The Lord to Ahab: "I will take away thy posterity" (1 Kings 21:21-24).
- (b) The Lord to Jehu: "Thou shalt smite the house of Ahab" (2 Kings 9:7-10).
- (c) The Lord about Jehu: "I will avenge the blood of Jezreel upon the house of Jehu" (Hosea 1:4).

44

Jehu could not have been blamed for wiping out all the house of Ahab, for that decree had been made by God. In fact, he was commended for the actual execution of God's decree (see 2 Kings 10:30). His guilt lay rather in the manner of his program and his heart attitude behind the murders. From your study of 10:1-17 and 10:18-27 what may be said of Jehu's heart?

Was his primary motive to do the will of God?

7. *See 10:18-27.* We must look here for a deeper sin other than Jehu's deception in luring the priests of Baal to their death. Do you see any possible *political* motive in Jehu's plot to destroy the Baal cult in Israel?

8. *See 10:28-31.* This paragraph reveals clearly that Jehu's religious purge of Baalism was not done out of a heart that was jealous for the law of God. Note the strength of the two words "howbeit" (v. 29) and "but" (v. 31).

9. *See 10:32-36.* From this paragraph we understand one reason for the divine appointment of Hazael as king of Syria. God used a foreign king—as He did on many occasions—to begin to "trim off" the land possessions of Israel. Note the phrase "began to" in verse 32. Does God accomplish all His purposes in a brief moment?

II. COMMENTS

A. Judah's King—Jehoram (2 Kings 8:16-24; 2 Chron. 21)

From 2 Kings 8:16 we see that for a time Joram, the son of Ahab, and Jehoram, the son of Jehoshaphat, were reigning simultaneously: Joram on the throne of Israel and Jehoram on the throne of Judah.

Although Jehoram was the son of one of the best of Judah's kings, he himself was one of the worst. Jehoram married Ahab's daughter Athaliah, an evil match that quickly deteriorated Jehoram's spiritual life to the point where he took on all the ways of evil King Ahab, including Baal worship (cf. 1 Kings 18:16-18; 2 Kings 8:18).

If there was a sin to be committed, Jehoram did it, including murder, idolatry, oppression, and blasphemy. Only God's promise to David saved the house of Jehoram from utter destruction. God had promised David to "make him and his sons a perpetual light" (2 Kings 8:19, *Berkeley*). That is, God promised a succession of kings from one generation to another, so that his family should not be extinct till it terminated in the Messiah. God kept this unconditional promise, regardless of the apostasy and sin of David's descendants. This explains God's forbearance with the kings of Judah. No matter how bad a king of Judah might be, his son was allowed to succeed him on the throne. In Israel it was not so. There dynasty after dynasty was cut off because of wickedness. God had made no unconditional promise to Jeroboam, the founder of the ten-tribe kingdom, regarding his descendants.

But while the dynasty of David was allowed to continue its sovereignty over Judah, the wickedness of the individual kings of Judah was by no means allowed to go unpunished.

Jehoram completely ruined the reforms that his good father and grandfather had carried out. Think of the people who, under Jehoshaphat had been encouraged and exhorted to the study of God's Word and to prayer and trust in Him, now under Jehoshaphat's son were actually being *compelled* to sin thus grievously. (See 2 Chron. 21:11.) And all this largely because of the influence of a bad woman—"For the daughter of Ahab was his wife" (2 Kings 8:18; see 2 Chron. 21:6).

The first chastisement that fell on Jehoram for forsaking the Lord God of his fathers was the revolt of some of his subjects, the Edomites, whom he vainly tried to subdue, and also the people of Libnah, a city in his own kingdom.

Then there was delivered to Jehoram a letter from Elijah, written before the prophet's translation, which he probably entrusted Elisha to deliver when the time should be ripe for such a rebuke from the Lord (2 Chron. 21:12-15.) However, Jehoram did not heed the message of this letter, and the next chastisement sent upon him was the invasion of the Philistines and the Arabians, with the consequent loss of much property, his wives, and all his sons except his youngest son, Jehoahaz.

Even this fearful punishment did not turn Jehoram from his wickedness, and there was sent upon him the dread disease that Elijah had prophesied. When he died he was unmourned by his people and was buried in disgrace. Although he was not allowed to be buried in the sepulchers of the kings, he was buried in the city of Jerusalem.

At the close of Jehoram's eight years of troublesome reign, filled with war, rebellion, bereavement, loss, and disease, his son Ahaziah became king, but only in name. His mother, Athaliah, really reigned over Judah, as did her mother, Jezebel, in the north over Israel. These two pagan women, who hated God and loved idolatrous wickedness with all their heart, held the reins of government in both the royal houses. So great was their influence that the national faith was in danger of being completely driven from the land and in its place the abomination of heathenism established. This was the critical situation that brought on the judgments that followed.

B. Judah's King—Ahaziah (2 Kings 8:25-29; 2 Chron. 22:1-7)

Ahaziah, who succeeded his father, Jehoram, on the throne of Judah was called by two different names. In 2 Kings 8:25 he is called Ahaziah, and in 2 Chronicles 21:17 he is called Jehoahaz. (The latter name differs from the former mainly by the addition of *Jeho*, which refers to the divine name *Jah*.)

Ahaziah was, like his father, a wicked man, but little else could be expected with such a father and such a mother and such counselors as he had. Fortunately his reign continued only about a year. His uncle Joram, his mother's brother, was king of Israel, and Ahaziah was induced to join with him in a war against Syria. Joram was wounded in the war and went to Jezreel to recover. It was there that Ahaziah visited his sick uncle, and it was there that he met his death by the hand of Jehu.

C. Israel's King—Jehu (2 Kings 9:1–10:36)

Read 1 Kings 19:15-17 and note that Jehu and Hazael had been chosen to be God's instruments in punishing and destroying the house of Ahab.

Elisha knew that the time had come for God to execute the doom that He had announced through Elijah against the house of Ahab (1 Kings 21:17-28). He also knew that Jehu was to be God's instrument. Accordingly he sent one of the young prophets to Ramoth-gilead to anoint Jehu and acquaint him with the judgment work he was to do. Sudden and unexpected as this announcement was, both Jehu and the captains seem to have acknowledged that the appointment was authoritative, and Jehu was hastily proclaimed king.

Jehu was destined to be one of the most conspicuous figures in the entire history of the northern kingdom. He was the founder of the fifth dynasty, a dynasty that was to continue 114 years, twice as long as any other in Israel. He was appointed to be the executioner of divine judgment upon Baal worshipers, especially upon the wicked house of Ahab.

Hardly any story of tragedy in the Bible is so graphically pictured as is the history of this king. From the moment the prophet appeared at Ramoth-gilead and delivered God's message, to the day that Jehu drove Baal worship out of Israel, it was one rapid succession of awful judgments upon idolatry.

Jehu was a man well qualified for the work appointed him, being bold, resolute, fearless, ambitious, and merciless. It required a man of iron nerve to wade through blood as Jehu did.

No sooner was he proclaimed king and became assured of the allegiance of the army than he disclosed his plan of conspiracy against King Joram. None but Jehu must leave the city of Ramoth-gilead that the army of Israel was holding against the Syrians. It was arranged that Jehu with a small company would ride into Jezreel, take the king by surprise, and there slay him and rule in his stead.

Back in Jezreel the two kings, Joram of Israel and Ahaziah of Judah, were unsuspecting of danger. Possibly when the watchman on the tower of Jezreel reported the approaching company, driving furiously as Jehu was known to drive, they may have thought that urgent news from the battlefield was being brought. Perhaps the Syrians had again taken Ramoth-gilead. Hastily they dispatched messengers and were utterly unprepared for what took place. Joram's hour had come, and Jehu slew him with bow and arrow.

Ahaziah, though king of Judah, was Ahab's grandson; and being also an idolater, he was within Jehu's commission. So, being found with Joram, he shared his punishment. "And the destruction of Ahaziah was of God" (2 Chron. 22:7).

The next to die was wicked Jezebel. She died as she had lived —proud, arrogant, defiant. Jezebel's reference to Zimri (2 Kings 9:31) is made plain by 1 Kings 16:8-10, 15-20. Her words to Jehu intimated that he would have a similar fate. Note to fulfillment of the prophecy spoken through Elijah by comparing 1 Kings 21:23 with 2 Kings 9:35-36.

Judgment on the house of Ahab is described in 2 Kings 10:1-17. What a horrible picture it presents. Not only the seventy sons of Ahab but all who pertained to the household of Ahab, his relatives, his "great men," and his priests were slain. And still the slaughter went on. Ahaziah's kinsmen were killed; and then Jehu proceeded to exterminate all Baal worshipers in the land.

What was really the motive that actuated Jehu in all this bloodshed? Was it a desire for God's glory that moved him, or was it some selfish ambition? Did his zeal for himself exceed his zeal for God?

Jehu's actions had only the appearance of fervency in God's service. We see Jehu furiously driving toward Jezreel, killing the two kings who came forth to meet him, pausing to toss Joram's body into Naboth's field. Also we see him going on through the city, his horses and chariot wheels passing over the body of Jezebel; ordering Ahab's seventy sons to be slain and their heads piled up at the gate of the city; and then proceeding to Samaria, assembling every Baal worshiper in Israel, and by a butchery of the priests of Baal ridding his kingdom with one blow of this abominable form of idolatry. Indeed, we hear Jehu boasting to Jehonadab of his zeal for the Lord, as they ride together into Samaria (2 Kings 10:15-16), and God commends him for having executed the commission that had been given him. But in spite of all that, his *heart* was not right with God. He "took no heed to walk in the law of the Lord God of Israel with all his heart: for he departed not from the sins of Jeroboam, which made Israel to sin" (2 Kings 10:31).

To a certain extent, Jehu had done well: he had abolished *Baal* worship. But he did not sponsor *true* worship. The golden calves were just as displeasing to God as was Baal worship, but Jehu did nothing toward removing them. The reason is plain. In establishing a new dynasty it quite suited his purpose and was a wise political measure to abolish Baal worship, the religion introduced by the preceding house. But calf worship was an entirely different thing. Since the founding of the northern kingdom, the calves had been the emblem of Israel's independence from Judah, and Jehu had no notion of bringing the people back to the true worship of God, for that would mean the loss of a kingdom for himself. Like many another ambitious man, he considered politics of more importance than obedience to God. Therefore he lost out, as we see from 2 Kings 10:31-33. Immediately following the statement that Jehu took no heed to walk in the law of the Lord, we read: "In those days the Lord began to cut Israel short" (2 Kings 10:32).

About half of Jehu's kingdom was soon given over into the hands of Hazael, king of Syria (2 Kings 10:32-33).

God faithfully carried out His unconditional promise to Jehu to place four generations of his descendants on the throne of Israel, but if Jehu had been out-and-out for God, as David was, how much more would God have done for him! He missed much blessing because of his own selfishness. Jehu's experience should be a warning to all who obey God only so far as it seems to be advantageous to themselves. And that is not real *obedience.*

III. SUMMARY

As a summary exercise, tell the story of these chapters, using the following key sentences as guidelines. Make spiritual applications along the way. (The key phrases are italicized.)

Jehoram "departed *without being desired*" (2 Chron. 21:20).

"Yet the Lord would not destroy Judah *for David his servant's sake*" (2 Kings 8:19).

Ahaziah "did evil . . . as did the house of Ahab: for he was the *son in law of the house of Ahab*" (2 Kings 8:27).

"I have anointed thee king over *the people of the Lord, even over Israel*" (2 Kings 9:6).

"*Ye know the man*, and his communication" (2 Kings 9:11).

"*What peace, so long as* the whoredoms of thy mother Jezebel and her witchcrafts are so many?" (2 Kings 9:22).

"So the house of Ahaziah *had no power to keep still* the kingdom" (2 Chron. 22:9).

"They shall not say, *This is Jezebel*" (2 Kings 9:37).

"*The Lord hath done that which he spake* by his servant Elijah" (2 Kings 10:10).

"Thus Jehu destroyed Baal out of Israel. *Howbeit . . .*" (2 Kings 10:28-29*a*).

"In those days the Lord *began to cut Israel short*" (2 Kings 10:32).

Davidic Line Preserved in Joash

The house of Ahab was destroyed and Baal worship was stamped out by Jehu in the northern kingdom. In the last lesson we saw that Jehu was God's instrument in bringing about this reform in Israel.

In this lesson we turn our attention to the southern kingdom and see how a reformation was effected there. Judah as well as Israel needed cleansing, for Baal worship had invaded even the precincts of the sacred city. Ahaziah, king of Judah, who continued to sponsor Baalism in Judah as did his father, Jehoram, had perished at the time Jehu took the throne of Israel, but Baal worship was not abolished in Judah until seven years later.

Ahaziah had sons, one of whom probably would have been immediately placed on the throne of Judah had not Athaliah, the queen mother, who was as ambitious and unscrupulous as Jezebel (and no doubt maddened at the way her much loved religion was being stamped out in the north) murdered her own grandchildren, together with all who had claims to the throne, and made herself queen. She promoted Baal worship throughout Judah with fanatical zeal.

But here, at 11:2, appears one of the most significant acts of God in the history of His people, in His preserving the Davidic line—one of Ahaziah's sons escaped the massacre. Joash, then only a few months old, was hidden in the Temple by his aunt, Jehosheba, wife of the high priest. There he was kept during the six years that Athaliah reigned (2 Kings 11:1-3; 2 Chron. 22:10-12).

The lamp of David was flickering and seemed almost ready to be extinguished. His line had only this one frail child as its representative. But God's promises can never fail. He had not forgotten His promise to David. His watchful eye was on that feeble infant; His holy Temple sheltered the boy; and His priests ministered to him, awaiting the time when he should be presented to the people as their king.

An observation of the narrative of 2 Kings may be cited here concerning a relationship not made prominent in the text. That is, that those were the last years of the period of "alliances" between Israel and Judah, before the two nations resumed a relationship of hostility and antagonism. This is represented on the accompanying chart.

RELATIONSHIPS BETWEEN THE COEXISTING KINGDOMS OF ISRAEL AND JUDAH

	1 KINGS 12 ANTAGONISMS	1 KINGS 16:29 ALLIANCES	2 KINGS 13:10 ANTAGONISMS 2 KINGS 17
KINGS OF ISRAEL →	931 JEROBOAM TO OMRI	874 AHAB TO JEHOAHAZ	798 722 JEHOASH TO HOSHEA
KINGS OF JUDAH →	931 REHOBOAM TO ASA	873 JEHOSHAPHAT TO JOASH	796 722 AMAZIAH TO AHAZ
	ABOUT 60 YEARS	ABOUT 75 YEARS	ABOUT 75 YEARS

It is because of the new relationship (antagonism) between Israel and Judah beginning at 13:10 that we are using 13:9 as the concluding verse of the passage of this lesson.

In Lesson 5 King Jehu of Israel was the main character; in this lesson King Joash of Judah is the main character.

I. ANALYSIS

As you read this passage, keep the accompanying chart before you as a help in seeing the progress of the narrative and the relationships of the various parts. Record a paragraph title for each paragraph shown. Note that a paragraph from 2 Chronicles (2 Chron. 24:15-22) is inserted into the 2 Kings sequence. This is the one part of the parallel account of 2 Chronicles that furnishes a major addition to the story. (As part of your study you should read all of 2 Chron. 22:10–24:27; most of it follows 2 Kings, with the above exception.)

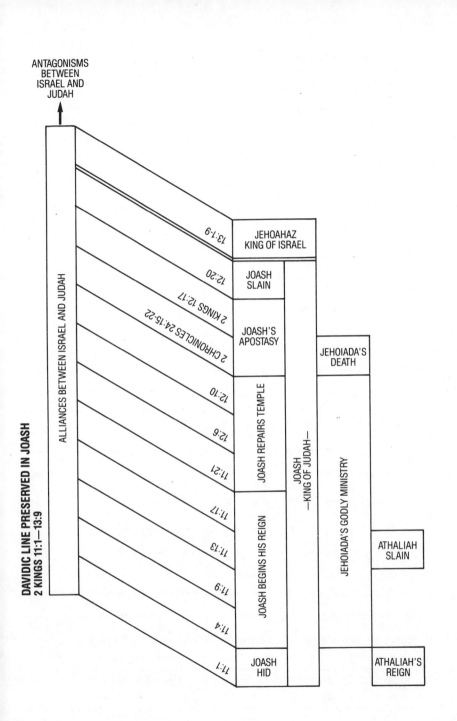

DAVIDIC LINE PRESERVED IN JOASH
2 KINGS 11:1—13:9

ANTAGONISMS
BETWEEN
ISRAEL AND
JUDAH

ALLIANCES BETWEEN ISRAEL AND JUDAH

13:1-9 — JEHOAHAZ KING OF ISRAEL

12:20 — JOASH SLAIN

2 KINGS 12:17

2 CHRONICLES 24:15-22 — JOASH'S APOSTASY

JEHOIADA'S DEATH

12:10

12:6

11:21 — JOASH REPAIRS TEMPLE

JOASH —KING OF JUDAH—

11:17

11:13

JEHOIADA'S GODLY MINISTRY

11:9 — JOASH BEGINS HIS REIGN

ATHALIAH SLAIN

11:4

11:1 — JOASH HID

ATHALIAH'S REIGN

53

1. *See 11:1-3.* Compare the two women Athaliah and Jehosheba. (In addition to the identifications given in 11:2, Jehosheba was also wife of the high priest Jehoiada, 11:4ff.)

Note any significance in the literal meanings of the names cited in this paragraph:

Athaliah	("Jehovah afflicts")
Ahaziah	("Jehovah hath grasped")
Jehosheba	("Jehovah is an oath")
Jehoram	("Jehovah is exalted")
Joash	("Jehovah supports")

Why would so many of the Bible names have the name Jehovah compounded in them?

2. *See 11:4-12.* What was the "testimony" that was given to Joash? (11:12).

What was the significance of this ritual?

3. *See 11:13-16.* Comment on the fact that it was a *high priest* who commanded the slaying of Queen Athaliah.

4. *See 11:17-20.* What important ministries were accomplished by the high priest in this paragraph?

Note the two descriptions of the people in 11:20.

Compare this with what had been originally promised the Israelites on their entrance into the land of Canaan (cf. Deut. 11:8-32).

5. *See 11:21–12:5.* How righteous was Joash's reign?

Notice the qualification introduced by "but" (v. 3). "Not idolatrous high places but illegal centers of Jehovistic worship. Notice 1 Kings 3:2. Only two kings of Judah, Hezekiah [2 Kings 18:4] and Josiah [23:8], removed the high places. One of the evil effects of this worship on the high places was that it divided Judah's spiritual vision; and thus it contributed materially to the nation's fall."[1]

Notice that it was the king who suggested a plan to finance the repair of the Temple. After that plan failed (v. 6), who offered a different plan? (v. 9).

6. *See 12:6-9.* This paragraph is introduced by another "but." What was the sin here, and who were the guilty ones? Read 2 Chronicles 24:5-6. What is the spiritual lesson for Christian workers today?

Notice that Jehoiada the high priest was still an active supporter of Joash as of this time.

7. *See 12:10-16.* Account for the generous offerings by the people.

Would God's work today lack finances if all of God's people were faithful stewards?

8. *See 2 Chronicles 24:15-22.* The key phrase describing Joash's apostasy is in 17*b*, "Then the king hearkened unto them." Analyze this paragraph as to what it reveals of Joash in his latter years. Joash's apostasy came after Jehoiada's death. What does this reveal about Jehoiada?

9. *See 2 Kings 12:17-19.* What was Joash's sin in this paragraph? (Cf. 2 Chron. 24:24.)

What was the judgment?

10. *See 12:20-21.* Compare 2 Chronicles 24:25 for the cause behind the slaying of Joash.

---

1. Charles F. Pfeiffer and Everett F. Harrison, eds., *The Wycliffe Bible Commentary* (Chicago: Moody, 1962), p. 351.

Note also the judgment concerning the place of his burial.

---

11. *See 13:1-9*. What does this paragraph teach about:
(a) sin and its judgment

(b) repentance and God's mercy

(c) return to sinful ways

---

12. What are three of the most important spiritual lessons you have learned from this passage?

II. COMMENTS

The contrast between the two women mentioned in 2 Kings 11:1-3 is great. Athaliah, the daughter of Ahab and Jezebel, was a very bad woman. Jehosheba, the daughter of King Jehoram and wife of Jehoiada the priest, was a very good woman. Athaliah was the instrument of Satan; Jehosheba the instrument of God. Back of Athaliah's unnatural deed of depravity, Satan was aiming at something of which his instrument was ignorant. "It was one of the many attempts Satan made to exterminate the male offspring to make the coming . . . [of] the promised Saviour, the seed of the woman, impossible. Had he succeeded through Athaliah in the destruction of the royal seed of David, the promise made to David would have become impossible [of fulfillment]."[2]

A. Judah's King—Joash (2 Kings 11:4–12:21; 2 Chron. 23:1–24:27)

It took only a few years for the nation to become profoundly dissatisfied with the depraved and callous queen who had thrust herself upon them, and the people were soon ready for almost any change. A woman governing them, and a pagan woman at that; Baal worship in the holy city; Solomon's glorious Temple neglect-

---

2. A. C. Gaebelein, *The Annotated Bible, Joshua-Chronicles* (New York: Publication Office "Our Hope," 1915), p. 330.

ed; Phoenician customs and practices introduced at court—all these were humiliating to a Hebrew, plus being calculated to arouse general indignation. Therefore, when the high priest instituted a revolution, he found the people enthusiastically ready to join him.

By thus skillfully dividing and stationing the royal guard, Jehoiada the priest prevented any possible harm to the infant king until he had been presented to the people and actually crowned and acclaimed.

The chagrin and rage of Athaliah on hearing the joyous applause of the multitudes over Joash were the signs for Jehoiada to proceed with her execution. Then followed the happy business of breaking up the Baal worship in Judah, the establishment of the new king, Joash, and the revival of the worship of Jehovah.

The reform in Judah was a contrast in every respect with that which took place in Israel seven years previously. In Israel the leader was at the head of the army, whereas in Judah the chief leader was at the head of the priesthood. Jehu's move had been largely in self-interest; Jehoiada had no other object in view than God's glory. Israel's reformation had been accomplished with much bloodshed, but in Judah we read of no deaths except those of Athaliah and Mattan, the priest of Baal.

In Israel the change wrought had been political to a great extent, but in Judah it was purely religious. In Israel there was a change in dynasty, but in Judah a usurper was dethroned and the rightful heir made king. Jehoiada's plan was as well laid as that of Jehu, but although all preparations were made in secret there was nothing of the element of deceit that had marked Jehu's. Though dissimilar in method, the results of the movements were the same in both kingdoms in regard to Baal worship. Both Israel and Judah were at last free from this form of idolatry, at least for a time.

However we must not fail to observe that in Judah there had not been the utter destruction of all Baal worshipers as there had been in Israel. Consequently, the small heathen party, though crushed for the time, again lifted its head and regained power after the death of Jehoiada, as we shall see later.

The reign of Joash began well and continued so as long as Jehoiada the priest lived and instructed the king. The most important work accomplished during Joash's reign was the repairing of the Temple, which had fallen into decay and had been broken by the wicked family of Athaliah. Notice that the plan made by the king for raising money for the Temple repairs failed. But the plan made by Jehoiada the priest was eminently successful, and the repairs were speedily accomplished.

When Jehoiada died at the great age of 130 and was buried with honor among the kings (2 Chron. 24:15-16), the nation lost a man of mighty influence for good.

King Joash was then more than thirty years of age. From earliest childhood he had been under the instruction of this good priest, so he ought to have been able to go on leading the people in the ways of God. But he appears to have been something of a weakling, easily flattered and easily influenced. He listened to the advice of the princes, who at heart were idolaters, and soon the house of the Lord was abandoned for groves and idols. Consequently the wrath of God was kindled against Judah and Jerusalem. God in His mercy sent them prophets, but the people would not listen to them (2 Chron. 24:17-19).

When Hazael king of Syria threatened Jerusalem, Joash did not call upon God for help. Instead, he stripped the Temple of its treasures and gave them to Hazael, who departed for a time, having been appeased by the bribe.

That Joash had become lost to all sense of reverence, honor, and gratitude is shown by his base command to stone to death in the Temple on the Day of Atonement the son of his benefactor, who endeavored to keep him back from his own ruin (2 Chron. 24:20-22).

The murder of the martyr priest was avenged. The year had not closed before all of those wicked princes lay dead, slain by Hazael king of Syria (2 Chron. 24:23-24). And then Joash was murdered by his own servants and denied burial in the sepulcher of the kings (2 Chron. 24:25-27).

B. Israel's King—Jehoahaz (2 Kings 13:1-9)

Chapter 13 of 2 Kings takes us back to the northern kingdom, and we first study the seventeen-year reign of Jehoahaz, son of Jehu.

God had promised that the line of Jehu would continue for four generations. Jehoahaz was the first of these four. Verse 2 describes the character of this king, and verses 3 to 7 tell the terrible punishment that God sent upon Israel for their sin.

III. SUMMARY

The story of these chapters interweaves the careers of Jehoiada, a priest of God, and Joash, a king of the house of David. How these two lives touched each other is shown by the accompanying summary chart.

JEHOIADA Priest of God	① His wife saves Joash	② His counsel helps Joash	③ His death marks the beginning of Joash's decline	④ His son slain by Joash
	↓	↓	↓	↓
JOASH King of Davidic line	INFANT Saved from massacre	YOUNG MAN Serves the Lord	MATURE MAN Sinks into apostasy	MARKED MAN Slain for murder

2 Kings 13:10–15:31
2 Chronicles 25:1–26:23

Recoveries of Israel
Before Captivity

Although the Kings passage of this lesson records the history of both Israel and Judah, the spotlight is on Israel. This is recognized by the full account devoted to Israel and, by way of contrast, in the omission of important facts about Judah from the narrative. (We know of these omissions from the parallel Chronicles passage, which incidentally records only facts concerning the kingdom of Judah.)

The title for this lesson therefore refers only to Israel. But since our study also involves the Chronicles passage, we shall observe some important truths about Judah as well. By way of anticipation, these are two prominent lessons that we shall learn in our study:

1. *Lesson from Israel*:

When the overall reigns of kings are evil, there may be temporary victories (granted in the grace of God), but ultimate doom is sure.

2. *Lesson from Judah*:

Overall reigns of kings may be good, but sins are still judged.

As you prepare to study this lesson, review the chronology of the kings of this lesson, as shown on the *Chart of Kings and Prophets* (pp. 110-11). These kings are listed in the accompanying chart. The arrows show the order in which they appear in the 2 Kings narrative.

Note the reference to Assyria on the chart. As you read the chapters of this lesson, follow the sequence of the kings on the *Chart of Kings and Prophets*. This will prove to be of great benefit to you.

I. ANALYSIS

For your first reading go through the Kings passage first; then read 2 Chronicles 25:1–26:23 to note especially the additions offered

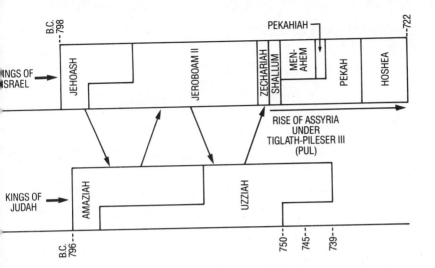

there. Make notations in your Bible as you read, for reference later on.

Next return to 2 Kings, analyzing the passage paragraph by paragraph. Record on the accompanying work sheet important items for each paragraph. Each observation you record should be kept brief, for clarity's sake. After you have done this, study the outlines shown on the work sheet and compare them with your own observations. Then answer the following questions.

1. Concerning the sequence Recoveries; Disintegration; Captivity, what has been the northern kingdom's history up till now, and what does the above sequence add to that?

_____

_____

_____

2. *See 13:10-13.* How is Jehoash's reign described here?

_____

_____

_____

3. *See 13:14-19.* What does verse 14 reveal of Jehoash's relationship to Elisha?

_____

_____

RECOVERIES OF ISRAEL BEFORE CAPTIVITY
2 KINGS 13:10—15:31

	ISRAEL	JUDAH	
	JEHOASH	AMAZIAH	
RECOVERIES	13:10	14:1	GOOD REIGN
	13:14		SIN OF IDOLATRY 2 Chronicles 25:14-16
		14:8	
	13:20		JUDGMENT OF DEFEAT
		14:17	
1. Recovery of territories	13:22		
	13:25	14:22	
2. Victory over Judah	JEROBOAM II	UZZIAH	
3. Recovery of territories	14:23	15:1	GOOD REIGN
			SIN OF PRESUMPTION 2 Chronicles 26:16-18
	14:29	15:7	JUDGMENT OF LEPROSY
DISINTEGRATION	15:8 ZECHARIAH		
DISINTEGRATING THRONE			
	15:13 SHALLUM		
	15:16 MENAHEM		
	15:23 PEKAHIAH		
CAPTIVITY	15:27 PEKAH		
FIRST DEPORTATION TO ASSYRIA (before 732 B.C.)	15:30 HOSHEA		
	15:31		

Compare 14*b* with Elisha's words of 2:12.

_____

What does the latter part of this paragraph reveal of the king's relationship to Elisha?

_____

(Note: The symbolism of the arrows demonstration was not uncommon at that time. "Jehoash knew very well what was being symbolized. He was probably unwilling to destroy Syria for the same reason as Ahab, i.e., fear of Assyria."[1]

4. *See 13:20-21.* What purpose did God accomplish by this miracle?

_____

The answer is not stated in the text; try to arrive at a plausible answer. Keep in mind that miracles were signs that demonstrated, in a particular setting and to those people observing, a specific relationship between (1) God and (2) the subject and/or the worker of the miracle.

5. *See 13:22-25.* Read verse 22 thus: "Now Hazael king of Syria had oppressed . . ." Recall that during Jehu's reign Hazael had captured the regions east of the Jordan (2 Kings 10:32-33); during Jehoahaz's reign Hazael took many of Israel's cities (cf. 13:3, 22, 25). Then came a day of temporary recovery. Did Jehoash utterly destroy Syria? (Compare the "three times" of v. 25 with v. 19.)

_____

What is the suggestion of the phrase "as yet" in verse 23?

_____

6. *See 14:1-7.* Compare 14:3 with 2 Chronicles 25:2.

_____

What does this paragraph reveal of Amaziah's reign?

_____

_____

1. F. Davidson, A. M. Stibbs, and E. F. Kevan, eds., *The New Bible Commentary* (Grand Rapids: Eerdmans, 1953), p. 324.

Note the familiar qualification of verse 4. How common was this of Judah's kings?

_____

_____

7. *See 2 Chronicles 25:14-16.* This paragraph reveals the cause of the judgments upon Amaziah recorded in 2 Kings 14:8ff.

8. *See 2 Kings 14:8-22.* Here are recorded the judgments upon Amaziah. What important lesson is to be learned from the life of Amaziah, of whom it was said that "he did right in the sight of the Lord" (with qualifications)?

_____

_____

9. *See 14:23-29.* What recoveries are cited here?

_____

_____

Account for the Lord's granting these to Israel.

_____

_____

10. *See 15:1-7.* The names Azariah (e.g., 15:1) and Uzziah (e.g., 15:13) refer to the same man. (Azariah—"Jehovah is help"—may have been his official name; Uzziah means "Jehovah is might.") Note the familiar qualification of verse 4 in evaluating the reign of Uzziah. Read 2 Chronicles 26:1-15 to note the many ways in which Uzziah prospered. Read 2 Chronicles 26:16-18 to learn the cause of the leprosy cited in 2 Kings 15:5. What was Uzziah's sin?

_____

Compare the sins of Amaziah and Uzziah, and their judgments.

_____

_____

11. *See 15:8-31.* Here begins the list of the last six kings of Israel, spanning a period of thirty-one years, an average of only five years per king. What evidence of disintegration do you observe in these paragraphs?

_____

_____

Note the two references to the king of Assyria. Pul (v. 19) and Tiglath-pileser II (v. 29) refer to the same king. The captivity of verse 29 was the first deportation of Israelites to Assyria, accomplished some time before 732 B.C. The second and final deportation (722 B.C.) would be the end of the kingdom.

12. From your study of this passage concerning the kings of the two kingdoms, list some of the major truths taught. Are such lessons from Old Testament kings applicable to living in the present age?

_____

_____

_____

_____

_____

II. COMMENTS

A. Israel's King—Jehoash (2 Kings 13:10-25)

Jehoash was the second of the four generations promised to Jehu. He, like his father, was a wicked man in that he followed the sins of Jeroboam the son of Nebat.

Jehoash himself was not a follower of God, and the calves of Dan and Bethel were still being worshiped during his reign. But he did not actively oppose the worship of Jehovah, and he seemed to appreciate Elisha's work. He looked upon Elisha as a great bulwark of the kingdom and mourned over his impending death.

Elisha encouraged the weeping king and assured him of victory over Syria by a symbolic act, using bow and arrows. It is as though Elisha had said, "I am dying, but the Lord still lives. Take courage because He will be with you as you war with Syria. This arrow speeding eastward is the arrow of the Lord's deliverance" (see 2 Kings 13:17). Then Elisha tested the zeal and faith of the king and found them faint. So only partial victory was promised. Even partial victory was of God's grace.

The time was coming and was not far distant when the ten tribes would be utterly cast aside by God and scattered throughout the nations; but God's forbearance and compassion had not "as yet" given out.

65

B. Judah's King—Amaziah (2 Kings 14:1-22; 2 Chron. 25:1-28)

Amaziah was a young man of twenty-five when he came to the throne, and he began his reign well. It is stated that he did that which was right in the sight of the Lord, yet not like David his father. God always looks at the heart; although Amaziah's acts during the first years of his reign were right, his heart was not perfect before God as David's had been.

That Amaziah had regard for the law of God at this time is seen in the fact that when he slew the servants who had murdered his father he did not slay their children, which God's law forbade. (Compare Deut. 24:16 with 2 Kings 14:1-6 and 2 Chron. 25:1-4.) Perhaps his knowledge of and respect for the law of God were due to his mother's influence. The good priest Jehoiada had chosen her to be the wife of Amaziah's father (2 Chron. 24:3), and it is not likely that that godly priest would have chosen anyone other than a woman of piety to be queen of Judah.

After having avenged his father's death, Amaziah opened war on Edom. (Locate Edom on the map.) Evidently Amaziah did not deem his own forces strong enough to subjugate the Edomites, because he hired 100,000 soldiers from Israel, which was about one-third as many as he had in his own army. For the services of these soldiers he paid one hundred talents of silver, estimated at $218,000 (2 Chron. 25:5-6, *Berkeley*).

Amaziah had made his arrangements for this war with Edom without consulting God, as is apparent by the message that God sent him. But that he was willing afterward to forfeit the $218,000 rather than act contrary to the Lord's command is much to his credit (2 Chron. 25:7-10). "Whenever believers face pecuniary losses on account of being true to the Lord and to His Word, they should remember that the Lord, who is thus honored, is able to make up for it and give much more."[2]

Amaziah's victory over the Edomites was complete and merciless. Meanwhile Israel's army, which had been sent back, avenged themselves for what they undoubtedly regarded as an insult by raiding the cities of Judah (2 Chron. 25:13).

That was the turning point in Amaziah's career. Not only did his successful campaign against Edom fill him with pride, but he became infatuated with the idols of Edom and actually become an idolater himself (2 Chron. 25:14). Then notice his attitude toward God's messenger. His idolatry and his refusal to heed God's rebuke brought on his ruin (2 Chron. 25:15-16).

2. A. C. Gaebelein. *The Annotated Bible, Joshua-Chronicles* (New York: Publication Office "Our Hope," 1915), pp. 452-53.

Filled with pride over his recent military victories and no doubt determined to avenge the damages done by Israel's rejected army, Amaziah next challenged Jehoash, king of Israel, to war. Perhaps in his vanity he thought to subjugate the kingdom of Israel, which was three times as large as his own, and reunite it with Judah. But the king of Israel, secure in his sense of superior numbers, treated Amaziah's challenge with disdain, answered him by a parable, and strongly advised him to remain at home and be content with the conquests he had already gained. Probably the "advice" that Amaziah took was that of his own statesmen.

In the parable by which Jehoash answered Amaziah, the king of Israel compared himself to a stately cedar and Amaziah to a thistle. The "wild beast" apparently referred to his own military forces that he felt confident could easily crush those of Judah. Amaziah's defeat was complete and was in punishment for his idolatry, as God had told him.

Although Amaziah lived fifteen years after the death of his conqueror, the king of Israel, they were barren years, so far as we have any record. From the time he departed from the Lord, the hearts of his subjects departed from him. A conspiracy was formed against him in Jerusalem, and when he fled to Lachish he was pursued and slain.

C. Israel's King—Jeroboam II (2 Kings 14:23-29)

Jeroboam II reigned longer than any other king of Israel. For forty years he occupied the throne (part of the time as co-regent with Jehoash), and during that time he restored the kingdom to a greatness that it had not attained since the reign of Solomon. And yet the Holy Spirit relates the whole history of his life in six short verses. "Man looketh on the outward appearance, but the Lord looketh on the heart" (1 Sam. 16:7*b*). As man looked at Jeroboam II, he was a great king; as God looked at him, he was a lost sinner (2 Kings 14:24). Outwardly the reign of Jeroboam II was most successful; inwardly it was an utter failure.

Look at the *Chart of kings and Prophets* and note that Amos, Hosea, and Jonah were prophesying in the days of Jeroboam II. Read some of their writings to see the depths of iniquity to which Israel had fallen.

In 2 Kings 14:25 it is stated that the military conquests of Jeroboam II were declared by the prophet Jonah to have been according to the word of the Lord, and the two following verses show the pity and the long-suffering of the Lord for His beloved people, even in their great sins.

67

D. Judah's King—Uzziah (Azariah) (2 Kings 15:1-7; 2 Chron. 26:1-23)

Uzziah is also called Azariah (2 Chron. 26:1-3; Isa. 1:1; 6:1). He was made king at the age of sixteen and reigned fifty-one years. His reign might be divided into two periods: the first, when he was obedient to God and prospered; the second, when he was disobedient to God and suffered punishment. The first period, however, is by far the longer of the two.

Uzziah owed his prosperity to God (2 Chron. 26:5). Note the several ways in which he was prosperous:

1. In his warfare (2 Chron. 26:6-8)

2. In his defenses (2 Chron. 26:9); these towers were for fortifying his capital

3. In his farming enterprises (2 Chron. 26:10)

4. In his armies (2 Chron. 26:11-15)

Now note the ominous word with which 2 Chronicles 26:16 begins. How often that little word "but" occurs in Scripture, even after much good has been said of an individual. This verse marks the beginning of the second stage in Uzziah's reign, that in which he was disobedient to God and suffered punishment.

Much prosperity and honor turned Uzziah's head. He seemed to think that nothing was too good for him and that he could do anything he liked. He boldly invaded the priest's office, in spite of the vehement protest of the priests, and insisted on burning incense in the Temple. This was indirect violation of the will of God as revealed through Moses. "The kingly and the priestly offices were separated by the law of God, not to be united again but in the person of the Messiah." King Uzziah's punishment was swift and awful.

Because Uzziah was a leper, his son Jotham judged the people (2 Chron. 26:21), and when he died he was buried without honors (2 Kings 15:5-7; 2 Chron. 26:21-23).

E. Israel's King—Zechariah (2 Kings 15:8-12)

Here begins the list of the last kings of Israel. Long and patiently God, through the prophets, had pleaded with the people to turn to Him, but to no avail. Soon He would plead no more.

Zechariah was the fourth and last ruler of the dynasty of Jehu. This evil reign was allowed to continue for only six months, and then Zechariah was assassinated by Shallum, who took the throne.

F. Israel's King—Shallum (2 Kings 15:13-15)

Shallum occupied the throne only one month when he met with the same treatment that he had accorded Zechariah. He was slain by Menahem, probably his military leader.

All was now in confusion, and there was political disorder in Israel. Conditions grew worse and worse until the end came.

G. Israel's King—Menahem (2 Kings 15:16-22)

Menahem was a particularly brutal and ferocious monarch, as evidenced by his treatment of the people of Tiphsah when that city refused to surrender to him.

For ten years he held the reins of government. It was during his reign that Assyria, the nation that God used a little later to execute judgment on the kingdom of Israel, made the first threatening advances. Assyria was bought off at this time for one thousand talents of silver ($2,000,000), which King Menahem raised by levying a tax upon the men of wealth in his kingdom. Some think that this amount was demanded by Assyria each year.

H. Israel's King—Pekahiah (2 Kings 15:23-26)

Pekahiah reigned only two years. His character was evil, like that of all the kings who had preceded him, and he was killed by Pekah, one of his captains.

I. Israel's King—Pekah (2 Kings 15:27-31)

Pekah reigned twenty years, and during his reign Assyria again advanced upon Israel, having left Syria in ruins. Galilee and all the land of Naphtali were conquered, and the Israelites inhabiting that territory were carried captive to Assyria.

Near the end of Pekah's reign, Hoshea, assisted by Tiglath-pileser, the Assyrian king, conspired against Pekah. Hoshea slew Pekah and reigned in his stead.

III. SUMMARY

While things were relatively quiet in the southern kingdom, unrest, wars, and murders in the north ominously spoke of approaching death for Israel. God in His grace granted some late victories for Israel to remind them of the covenant that He had made with Abraham and which they were haughtily violating. But these victories were only like the temporary deathbed rally of a dying man, and before long the nation was plunging headlong to destruction. The first and partial deportation of Israelites to Assyria, as studied in this lesson, is the harbinger of the total captivity a decade or so later, which is the story of the next lesson.

Lesson 8

Judah in Trouble
and Israel Taken Captive

Chapter 17 of 2 Kings is a key chapter for it records the tragic end of the northern kingdom. Recall from the survey chart of 2 Kings (p. 7) how chapter 17 is a critical junction in the narrative of the book. The accompanying chart is an excerpt from the survey chart.

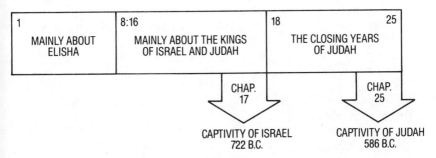

1	8:16	18	25
MAINLY ABOUT ELISHA	MAINLY ABOUT THE KINGS OF ISRAEL AND JUDAH	THE CLOSING YEARS OF JUDAH	

CHAP. 17 → CAPTIVITY OF ISRAEL 722 B.C.

CHAP. 25 → CAPTIVITY OF JUDAH 586 B.C.

The section just before chapter 17 (15:32–16:20) describes the situation in Judah at the time her sister nation was carried into captivity by the Assyrians. As the title of this lesson indicates, our present study is of two parts: Judah in trouble, and Israel taken captive.

I. ANALYSIS

A. Judah in Trouble (2 Kings 15:32–16:20; 2 Chron. 27:1–28:27)

First read about the reign of Jotham in 2 Kings 15:32-38 and 2 Chronicles 27.
What kind of king was Jotham?

How is he likened to his father Uzziah?

_____

_____

What big sin of Uzziah was Jotham not guilty of? (Cf. 2 Chron. 27:2 and 26:16 to understand the reference "Howbeit he entered not into the temple of the Lord.")

_____

Notice the familiar "howbeit" of 2 Kings 15:35. What does this tell you about Jotham?

_____

Were Jotham's subjects pleasing to the Lord by their living?

_____

Refer to the *Chart of Kings and Prophets* and note that the prophets Isaiah, Micah, and Hosea (and probably many other prophets whose words are not preserved) were preaching and teaching during this period. But in spite of the good example of the king and the good instruction of the prophets, the people of Judah persisted in sin.

The condition of the people and their attitude toward God is told by the prophet Isaiah in the first five chapters of his book. These chapters should be read in order to understand the conditions existing at that time.

Judah as well as Israel was treasuring up wrath against the day of wrath and punishment that was to overtake her. This began to be felt in the days of Jotham.

Notice the *beginning* of the Lord's test referred to in 2 Kings 15:37. What was the Lord's purpose in this test?

_____

_____

Judah failed the test under their next king, Ahaz, as chapter 16 reveals.

Now study carefully 2 Kings 16 and 2 Chronicles 28. Observe the similarities and differences of the two chapters. Record on the accompanying work sheet the main items you observe in your study of each paragraph shown.

1. Notice the similarity of the opening phrase of 2 Kings 15:32 and 16:1. Compare the two kings Jotham and Ahaz.

_____

_____

SINS AND
JUDGMENTS

KEY WORDS
AND PHRASES

KEY
EVENTS

2 CHRONICLES 28:1-8
2 CHRONICLES 28:9-15
2 CHRONICLES 28:16-21
2 KINGS 16:10-20
2 CHRONICLES 28:22-27

2. See 2 Chronicles 28:1-8. What verses describe Ahaz's sins, and what verses describe the judgments?

_____

_____

Read Isaiah 7 in connection with this paragraph.
3. See 2 Chronicles 28:9-15. What was the basis of Oded's appeal for the release of the children of Judah?

_____

_____

What does this paragraph teach about sin?

_____

What does it teach about God's sovereign use of instruments for His purposes?

_____

4. See 2 Chronicles 28:16-21. What was Ahaz's sin in verse 16?

_____

In verse 19?

_____

In verse 21?

_____

From verse 19, what do you learn about the destructive influence of a leader upon his followers?

_____

Did Ahaz get the help he sought?

_____

What does this teach?

_____

5. See 2 Kings 16:10-20. This paragraph shows the corruption to which Ahaz stooped in his defiance of God. Not only did he go after other gods, but he desecrated the things of God's Temple. For example:

_____

_____

6. See 2 Chronicles 28:22-27. According to verses 22-23, what was Ahaz's concept of worship?

_____

What constitutes true worship of God?

_____

Why should we worship God?

_____

_____

B. Israel Taken Captive (2 Kings 17)

This key chapter may be divided into two parts: Samaria Conquered (vv. 1-23); and Samaria Reinhabited (vv. 24-41). Observe from the accompanying analytical charts that each part may be divided into three paragraphs. Note the brief outlines shown on the charts. After you have read the chapter a few times, record your observations of key words and phrases and the relationships between them. This will give you a comprehensive view of the contents of this chapter.

2 KINGS 17

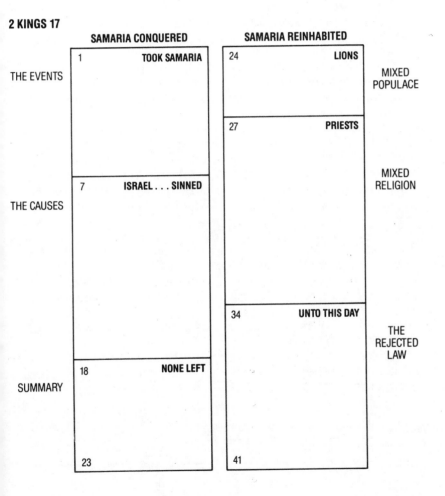

SAMARIA CONQUERED

1. *See 17:1-6.* Notice the reference to *degree* of evil in verse 2, as Hoshea's reign is compared with the more evil reigns of the kings before him. Observe how matter-of-fact is the record of the fall of Samaria, in verse 6.

Does the text record how many people were taken captive to the regions of the Assyrian Empire?

At least we may confidently assume that a large number of Israelites were taken captive. Consider the following:

(a) The purpose of deportation was not captivity for every individual but captivity of a multitude large enough so as to destroy the nation as a political unity and military force.

(b) The conquerors usually let the weak, poor, and powerless individuals remain in the land, partly to keep the fields in cultivation. Compare Jeremiah 39:10 as it applied to the captivity of Judah.

(c) The reference in 17:6 to Samaria is probably to the city, not the region, of Samaria. In this connection there was discovered in 1843 an inscription on the walls of the royal palace of Sargon by the king who actually took Samaria soon after Shalmaneser's death. This inscription reads in part: "I besieged and captured Samaria, carrying off 27,290 of the people who dwelt therein . . ."[1]

(d) The religious history of the new Samaritan "nation" after Israel's fall points to the fact that it originated in a mixture of Hebrew and imported foreign stock (cf. 17:24).

(e) The phrase "there was not left" of 2 Kings 17:18 has reference to tribes, not to individuals. The phrase "all the seed of Israel" of verse 20 would have to be interpreted in a collective sense. Most Bible scholars agree that some native Israelites were allowed to remain in the land.

2. *See 17:7-17.* The indictment against Israel is made clear here. Make a list of the different *kinds* of sins of which the Israelites were guilty.

---

1. Merrill F. Unger, *Unger's Bible Handbook* (Chicago: Moody, 1966), p. 233.

Notice also references to opportunities afforded them to repent of their sins.

---

3. *See 17:18-23*. Notice the key phrase of judgment, "out of his sight." What is meant by this?

Observe the two references to judgment:
    (a) Earlier, Israel was rent from Judah (v. 21).
    (b) Now, Israel is removed from the sight of God (vv. 20, 23).
If judgment for sin comes in this life in "steps," in what way does this suggest that we should learn from one judgment so as not to reap the next?

SAMARIA REINHABITED

4. *See 17:24-26*. In what way might the new dwellers of Samaria be called a mixed populace?

Who are the ones speaking the words of verse 26?

---

5. *See 17:27-33*. What is the significance of the king's words "The God of the land" (v. 27)?

What kind of a religion is described by the words "They feared the Lord, and served their own gods" (v. 33)?

---

6. *See 17:34-41*. Why does the author of 2 Kings include this paragraph?

What is it mostly about?

Observe especially the many references to the grace of God in His relationship to His people. Were they without excuse for their sin?

_____

_____

Notice the three opening and the three closing words.

7. Think back over the entire chapter and write out a list of important truths it teaches.

_____

_____

_____

_____

II. COMMENTS

A. Judah in Trouble (2 Kings 15:32–16:20; 2 Chronicles 27:1–28:27)

1. *King Jotham*

Except for the fact that Jotham allowed the "high places" to remain in the land, his reign was an exceptionally good one. He was a great builder and was successful in war; and the reason he became so mighty was that "he prepared his ways before the Lord his God" (2 Chron. 27:6).

But Jotham's people continued in their corrupt ways and heeded neither the example of their king nor the warnings and exhortations of such prophets as Isaiah, Micah, and Hosea. It was during the years of Jotham's reign that God began to send invading armies from Israel and Syria against them to show them their impotency because of their sinful ways. It was during the reign of Jotham's successor, Ahaz, that Judah found herself in deep trouble.

2. *King Ahaz*

Ahaz had a good father and a good son, but he himself was one of the worst kings Judah ever had. His father, Jotham, "did right in the sight of the Lord all the days of his life," which is high praise indeed. But Ahaz went to the other extreme. He seemed infatuated with every form of evil. Whatever he could do to provoke the Lord God to wrath, he did.

Note how he patterned his life after the kings of Israel. He followed after all kinds of heathen idolatry, made molten images for Baalim, and even sacrificed his own children to idols (2 Kings 16:1-4; 2 Chron. 28:1-4). Yet the Lord condescended to plead with Ahaz that he put his trust in Him. This we learn from the prophet Isaiah.

This was a critical time in the affairs of the kingdom of Judah. Even during Jotham's reign, clouds had begun to gather on the political horizon in the shape of a military combination of Syria and Israel against Judah, and now in Ahaz's reign these two kingdoms united in their efforts to conquer Ahaz and put a man of their own choosing on the throne of Judah (Isa. 7:1-6). Observe that they were threatening to exterminate the house of David. Consequently God had to act. He would not allow them to carry out this plan or to invade Jerusalem at this time, although the king of Syria did recover Elath (2 Kings 16:5-6).

God sent a message to the frightened king, assuring him that the plans of the two confederate kings to drive him from his throne would not be carried out—and pointing out the consequences to himself of refusing to believe in God (Isa. 7:5-9). Ahaz might have had God for an ally against the enemies who threatened him, if only he had turned to Him and trusted Him. But Ahaz would not do this, so God showed him how helpless he was to fight against Syria and Israel in his own strength. The multitudes of captives taken by the king of Syria (2 Chron. 29:5) were lost to Judah, but through the intercession of God's prophet Oded the two hundred thousand captives taken by the king of Israel were returned (2 Chron. 28:8-15).

Oded was an exceptionally bold, brave prophet. To give such a message of rebuke to an army flushed with victory needed courage indeed.

From 2 Chronicles 28:12-13 it is evident that some in Israel realized that they had sinned against God and had provoked His wrath by their iniquity.

Neither God's message through Isaiah, nor His chastisement of Ahaz by the confederate kings, caused this wicked monarch to turn to the Lord. When Syria and Israel again threatened him, instead of calling upon God for assistance he called upon Tiglath-pileser, king of the great eastern power Assyria. (Locate Assyria on the map, p. 9) The prophet Isaiah strongly advised against this alliance with the king of Assyria. He showed Ahaz that instead of really helping him permanently Assyria would eventually overcome Judah (Isa. 7:17-20). This great statesman-prophet, speaking with the knowledge that God had given him, exhorted the king and the people to seek for help, not from Assyria, nor from Egypt, as some proposed, but from almighty God.

Because Ahaz would not heed the prophet's words, his troubles multiplied. Not only Syria and Israel but also the Edomites and the Philistines oppressed him, and God allowed them to do so (2 Chron. 28:16-19).

God's warning through Isaiah that the king of Assyria would be Judah's conqueror rather than her helper was shown to be true. Tiglath-pileser did indeed hearken unto Ahaz and went up against Damascus (2 Kings 16:9), but he did not stop with that. After conquering Syria he went on into Judah, not to help but to distress Ahaz. The tribute that he demanded was so great that Ahaz stripped the house of God and the palace to meet it (2 Chron. 28:20-21).

One would think that after Ahaz's hopes of assistance from Assyria were blasted, and he was helpless before his enemies, that he would at last turn to the true source of help—his God. But no. For we read, "In the time of his distress did he trespass yet more against the Lord" (2 Chron. 28:22).

See how he went deeper and deeper into sin. See how persistently he followed after idolatry, and how irreverently he dealt with the house of the Lord (2 Chron. 28:23-35). One of the worst of his acts was to set aside the altar of God and put in its place another altar, a copy of a heathen one (2 Kings 16:10-18).

Ahaz's life was short. He began reigning at the age of twenty and died at thirty-six. He died as he had lived, and his death and the accession of his good son Hezekiah was a boon to the kingdom (2 Kings 16:19-20; 2 Chron. 28:26-27).

B. Israel Taken Captive (2 Kings 17)

Hoshea was the last ruler of the northern kingdom, and at the close of his short reign the ten tribes were carried away into captivity by the Assyrians. Thus ended the history of that kingdom, ruled by evil kings for about two hundred years.

The *immediate* cause that brought on the kingdom's overthrow was Hoshea's conspiracy against the king of Assyria to whom he had become a vassal some time before. Not willing to continue paying the tribute exacted by Assyria, Hoshea sought to make an alliance with the king of Egypt and thus free himself from the Assyrian yoke. Upon hearing of this, the king of Assyria made Hoshea a prisoner. Then he went throughout all the land of Israel with his army and made himself master of it. Samaria, the capital city, proved hard to conquer, but after a three-year siege he took it and carried away the people of Israel to Assyria, where he located them in different places.

The *underlying* cause of Israel's overthrow was their persistent sin of rejection of God. In 2 Kings 17 a review of the moral history of Israel is given, summarizing the sins that led to their downfall. Usually in human writings the downfall of a people is attributed to unwise management, weak leadership, or the superior strength of a conquering people, but in God's Book He does not emphasize these *secondary* causes but the *first* cause—sin. It was God who removed Israel out of their land, whoever were His instruments. As you study the books of Kings and Chronicles, constantly bear in mind the truth stated in Daniel 4:17, that "the most High ruleth in the kingdom of men, and giveth it to whomsoever he will, and setteth up over it the basest of men."

God's arraignment of His apostate people, recorded in 2 Kings 17:7-23, is a full one. God had designed Israel, together with Judah, to stand out among all the nations of the earth as His representative people, His instrument by which He might acquaint other nations with Himself. But when Israel had fully demonstrated their rejection of this high calling, God rejected them and removed them out of His chosen land, scattering them among the nations of the East.

Chapter 17 of 2 Kings also records the colonization of the region of Samaria after the Israelites had been deported. The king of Assyria transplanted into the land remnants of several peoples whom he had conquered. These foreign people were the ancestors of the Samaritans, of whom we read in the gospels. The mongrel character of their religion in which they "feared the Lord, and served their own gods" (17:33) is difficult to imagine. But such is the religion today of the professing Christian who acknowledges the Lord only in an external way while in heart and deed he denies Him as God.

If you are interested in studying the subsequent history of this mixed race of Samaritans until New Testament times, refer to a Bible dictionary.

The subsequent history of the ten tribes is a blank. The tribes have never been restored to Palestine as a people, although individuals came back after the Babylonian captivity of Judah, and there is a nation of Israel today. But according to the prophets, a day is coming when both Israel and Judah as a united kingdom shall again inherit the land of their fathers that God gave to Abraham and his descendants forever.

III. SUMMARY

The doom of Israel was inevitable, because Israel persisted in defying God and walking after other gods. God was long-suffering in withholding judgment from the nation, when one considers that for the two hundred years of their existence all the kings and most of the people did that which was evil in the sight of the Lord.

The whole land of Canaan had been given to the Israelites as a gift from God, and a generation of believers took up residence in the land when Joshua was their leader. Internal troubles soon caused a split in the kingdom, and the northern tribes, known as Israel, began their downward plunge to annihilation.

Then the day of judgment came; God scattered His people around the lands of Assyria; and Israel as a nation was no more.

Lesson **9**

Hezekiah's Reforms

With the fall and captivity of the northern tribes, the kingdom of the south was left alone to perpetuate a testimony for God. Ahaz, co-regent with Hezekiah[1] over Judah at the time of Israel's fall, could not champion God's cause because he was an evil king. But Hezekiah, his son, was a God-fearing young man and truly God's king of the hour.

Both politically and religiously the situation was dark when young Hezekiah took over Judah.

Ahaz had shut up the Temple during his wicked reign, forbidding the worship of Jehovah and filling the land with idols and false religions. By his alliance with Tiglath-pileser he had made Judah a tributary of Assyria. Judah had been weakened in war with Syria and thus had no strength in herself to meet Assyria, a powerful enemy with overwhelming numbers.

There were those in Judah who advocated making an alliance with Egypt to help beat back the Assyrian power that was pushing at its eastern boundaries. Others in Judah just as earnestly advised surrender to Assyria as a means to escape further bloodshed and suffering. But Isaiah, the fearless prophet of God, boldly raised his voice in uncompromising denunciation of both these policies and steadfastly pointed the people to Jehovah as their only source of strength and victory. Fortunately for the nation, the young king was in closest sympathy with all Isaiah taught.

1. The dates of the reign of Hezekiah have posed difficult problems for Bible scholars. Some hold that Hezekiah was co-regent with Ahaz at the time of the fall of Israel. See Charles F. Pfeiffer and Everett F. Harrison, eds., *The Wycliffe Bible Commentary* (Chicago: Moody, 1962), pp. 357-58. Others maintain that he began his reign around 715 B.C., without a co-regency. See Edwin R. Thiele, *The Mysterious Numbers of the Hebrew Kings*, rev. ed. (Grand Rapids: Eerdmans, 1965), pp. 118ff. As shown by the *Chart of Kings and Prophets*, this manual follows the view of a co-regency.

These three main influences might have delivered Judah from the fate already suffered by Israel: (1) the example of Israel's fate and a similar threat of foreign invaders, (2) the reform programs of Judah's kings, (3) and the ministries of the prophets.

1. *The example of Israel*

Israel's captivity by a foreign power was really a judgment for Israel's sins against God. Israel worshiped other gods, so did not look to God for deliverance from Assyria. Was Judah guilty of the same sins? The threat from outside was a situation similar to that of Israel's. The accompanying chart shows the names of some of the foreign kings that play a part in the remaining narrative of 2 Kings.

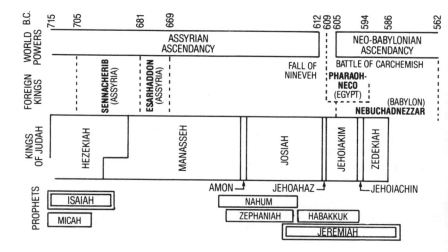

You may want to compare this chart with the *Chart of Kings and Prophets* (pp. 110-11) for dates, etc.

2. *The reform programs of Judah's kings*

There were two good kings of the surviving kingdom of Judah: Hezekiah and Josiah. Both instituted extensive religious reforms, though the benefits were only temporary. Your study of this present lesson centers mainly on Hezekiah's reforms.

3. *The ministries of the prophets*

The prophets are shown on the accompanying chart. Isaiah and Jeremiah were the key prophets of this period. Their message was mainly one of denunciation of sin and warning of judgment. It

84

could not be said of Judah, as it also could not be said of Israel, that the people were not given many warnings to repent of their evil ways.

I. ANALYSIS

Read through the passages (2 Kings 18:1-9 and 2 Chron. 29:1–31:21) for first impressions. Notice by comparison how brief the Kings passage is. What is the author's main purpose in recording this paragraph?

_____

_____

Let us study this paragraph (2 Kings 18:1-9) a little further at this time, following these suggestions:
1. Observe the author's evaluation of Hezekiah's reign in verse 3. Note the reference to and compare these verses: 1 Kings 15:3, 11; 2 Kings 14:3; 16:2; 22:2.

_____

_____

2. Recall the qualifying description "Howbeit the high places were not removed," which was assigned to most of Judah's kings before Hezekiah. What is said here about Hezekiah in this connection?

_____

Recall from your previous studies that whereas there was a worship of the true Jehovah at these places (cf. 2 Kings 18:22), the very existence of the places served to divide the spiritual fellowship of God's people. Only Hezekiah and Josiah (2 Kings 23:8) removed these high places.
3. Analyze the other good things said about Hezekiah, especially in verses 4-7.

_____

Now study 2 Chronicles 29-31 to learn all that Hezekiah did to restore a true worship of God to the land of Judah. Examine each section according to the following outline and identify what each paragraph is recording. Choose key words and phrases in each paragraph. Record all your observations.

1. *Cleansing of Levites*
   2 Chronicles 29:1-11
              29:12-19
2. *Offerings*
              29:20-24
              29:25-30
              29:31-36
3. *Passover* (Read Deut. 16:16; Lev. 23:5; Num. 9:9-11)
              30:1-5
              30:6-12
              30:13-22
4. *Purge of the land*
              31:1
5. *Appointments for Temple services*
              31:2-10
              31:11-19
6. *Summary*
              31:20

What are your impressions of Hezekiah's reforms?

_____

_____

_____

Were Hezekiah's motives right?

_____

Did the people respond favorably?

_____

What qualities and activities have many local churches of our present day lost or disowned?

_____

_____

In such cases, what can be done to urge revival?

_____

_____

What determines how lasting are the fruits of revival?

_____

_____

List other spiritual lessons taught by these chapters.

_____

_____

_____

_____

II. COMMENTS

It is significant that so many pages in the Bible are devoted to the twenty-nine years of Hezekiah's reign: three full chapters in 2 Kings, four chapters in 2 Chronicles, and parts of several chapters in Isaiah. This was a critical time in Judah's history, and Hezekiah was one of Judah's greatest kings.

Hezekiah's character is described in words that are used of only one other king of Judah (Asa): "He did that which was right in the sight of the Lord, according to all that David his father did." Those last eight words are omitted in the description of the other kings.

Having a heart like that of David, Hezekiah fully realized, as did Isaiah, that absolutely the only hope for the nation was a return to God in simple faith and implicit obedience to His word. This Isaiah preached up and down the land, backed always by the approval of King Hezekiah. But how impractical and fanatical this counsel must have appeared to the statesmen who were advising their own worldly-wise policies. In all ages during times of distress the majority of men trust in human devices rather than in divine means.

What do the politicians and statesmen of our own day advise in a crisis similar to the one that Judah was facing? If our own nation were threatened by an enemy so powerful that resistance seemed useless, would not the majority advise alliance with another nation? If a prophet should arise preaching as Isaiah did, what would the majority of the people think of the wisdom of following his suggestions?

The first thing that Hezekiah did on becoming king was to throw open the doors of the house of God and repair them, thus announcing that his purpose was to revive the worship of God and to make it his business to promote it.

The next thing he did was to call together the priests and the Levites to instruct and exhort them. In his speech to them he emphasized the necessity for cleansing, pointing out that it was sin that had brought about such a deplorable state of affairs in the kingdom. The obedient response of the Levites is heartening to read.

The cleansing of the Temple was immediately followed by the restoration of the Temple worship, as it had been appointed by David. Then, after the sanctifying and the worship, came the abundant giving.

This blessed turn of affairs was so speedily brought about within the first few weeks of Hezekiah's reign that it was plain that the Lord's hand was in it. God had secretly prepared the hearts of the people by the influence of His grace (2 Chron. 20:36).

Chapter 30 of 2 Chronicles tells of the great Passover that was kept at that time. The appointed time for the Passover was in the first month (Lev. 23:5). But since that time had passed, the king and the people, after conference together, resolved to take advantage of a special provision in the law of Moses (Num. 9:9-11) to keep the Passover in the second month.

Invitations to this Passover were sent out by messengers, not only throughout Judah but to all the cities and villages of Israel, although at that time many of the people of the ten tribes had been taken captive to Assyria. Hezekiah seemed passionately desirous that those who were left of the sister kingdom, as well as all the inhabitants of Judah, should return wholeheartedly to the Lord (2 Chron. 30:1, 5-9).

Although most of the invitations that Hezekiah sent to the northern kingdom were refused with ridicule and scorn, nevertheless some of the people of Israel humbled themselves, repented of their sins, and went to Jerusalem. From Judah the people went en masse, so that there was a large gathering at Jerusalem (2 Chron. 30:10-14). The "altars" referred to in verse 14 are those that Ahaz had made (2 Chron. 28:24).

In this hastily arranged celebration some things were necessarily done that were not in strict accordance with the instructions given through Moses for observing the Passover. For example, the Levites assisted in killing the offerings for the people (v. 17). Many who were not ceremonially clean were allowed to eat the Passover, because they prepared their hearts to seek God (2 Chron. 30:18-20).

The seven-day feast of unleavened bread followed the Passover. This was a great meeting. For the first time since the division of the kingdom under Rehoboam, both Judah and Israel were assembled at Jerusalem to worship God in the Temple. There was much gladness and singing and praise to God. There were prayers of confession and the offering of peace offerings. There was preaching and teaching by the Levites that was fully approved and commended by the king. Altogether there was so much blessing that it was agreed to extend the time of the meeting another seven days, and at the close of this second week the congregation was dismissed with the blessing and prayers of the priests and Levites.

Note that this zeal and enthusiasm was not over when the great meeting at Jerusalem closed. The people went forth from the place of blessing to put away the things offensive to God throughout the land.

Hezekiah was most desirous that all things should be in accordance with the law of God. He therefore revived and restored the courses of the priests and Levites (2 Chron. 31:2-3). Furthermore, he ordered that the long-neglected tithe be paid, that the service of the house of God might prosper. This order met with prompt and hearty response from the people (2 Chron. 31:4-10).

Hezekiah then wisely and systematically provided for the care and distribution of the gifts that the people had brought, so that none would feel that anything he contributed was wasted through neglect or carelessness. Certain men were appointed to take charge of these matters, each one in his proper place (2 Chron. 31:11-19).

All that Hezekiah did was with zeal, sincerity, and thoroughness, and he did it all as unto the Lord. It is no wonder that he prospered and was victorious over his enemies.

III. SUMMARY

The author of Chronicles has written verses in his account that vividly summarize the revival in Judah under Hezekiah. As a summary exercise, study these verses carefully: "So the service of the house of the Lord was set in order" (2 Chron. 29:35). "So there was great joy in Jerusalem: for since the time of Solomon the son of David king of Israel there was not the like in Jerusalem" (2 Chron. 30:26). "And thus did Hezekiah throughout all Judah, and wrought that which was good and right and truth before the Lord his God. And in every work that he began in the service of the house of God, and in the law, and in the commandments, to seek his God, he did it with all his heart, and prospered" (2 Chron. 31:20-21).

Lesson 10
Hezekiah's Trials

2 Kings 18:9–20:21
2 Chronicles 32:1-33

The reign of Hezekiah, one of Judah's greatest kings, was not without its testings and trials, which are the subjects of our present lesson. In Lesson 9 we studied Hezekiah's character and religious activities; now we shall give attention to his political and private life.

I. ANALYSIS

A. Invasions of Sennacherib (2 Kings 18:9–19:37; 2 Chron. 32:1-23; Isa. 36:1–39:8)

Read the passages first for orientation and initial impressions. As you read, underline words and phrases in your Bible that appear prominent and call for further study. Since Kings gives a more extended description of this story than Chronicles, our study will concentrate on the former. The Chronicles account should be used for what additional information it records along the way. (The Isaiah account is practically the same as Kings.) Use the following outline and the suggestions for study.

1. *First Invasion (2 Kings 8:13-16)*
Note by 8:7 that some time early in Hezekiah's reign he discontinued paying tribute to Assyria, an arrangement that his father, Ahaz, had agreed to. In addition to this, in 705 B.C., at the death of King Sargon II of Assyria, Hezekiah had entered into a secret alliance with Egypt against the power of Assyria (cf. Isa. 30:1-5 and 31:1-3). In light of all this, account for his words "I have offended," in 8:14.

Is there any indication from this paragraph that Hezekiah was trusting in God for help against Sennacherib?

Note the simple record of verse 13, that Sennacherib conquered all the fenced cities of Judah.

2. *Later Invasion (2 Kings 18:17–19:37; 2 Chron. 32:1-23)*
This campaign by the king of Assyria, thirteen years after the first one, ended in victory for Judah. Kings and Chronicles make clear that God delivered Judah because Judah looked to Him for help.

The position of this manual is that the campaign described by 2 Kings 18:17-37 is later than that of 8:13-16.[1] The consequences for Judah were different in each case. Since 2 Chronicles 32 refers to the later campaign, look for differences between these verses: 2 Chronicles 32:1 and 2 Kings 18:13.

(a) Challenge (2 Kings 18:17-35). Analyze carefully the various ways in which the Assyrian king, through his emissaries, tried to lure the people of Judah from their loyalty to Hezekiah and to God. Record your observations.

Notice references to these sources of trust: Egypt (18:21), God (18:22), Assyria (18:23), and gods of other nations (18:33-35).
(b) Reactions.
1. *The people* (2 Kings 18:36-37). Was silence wise action here?

2. *Hezekiah appeals to Isaiah* (2 Kings 19:1-7). Hezekiah sought help from "the house of the Lord" (v. 1) and from the prophet of God (v. 2). What does this reveal about his trust?

3. *Hezekiah prays to God* (2 Kings 19:8-19). Hezekiah's prayer was born of the arrogant letter from Sennacherib, which called God a

1. See C. F. Pfeiffer and E. F. Harrison, eds., *The Wycliffe Bible Commentary* (Chicago: Moody, 1962), p. 358, for further explanation.

deceiver (v. 10). On what things did Hezekiah base his plea for deliverance (vv. 15-19)?

___

4. *God's answers* (2 Kings 19:20-34). Write out some of the main things God told Sennacherib (vv. 21-28) and Hezekiah (vv. 29-34).

___

(c) Outcome (2 Kings 19:35-37).
"And it came to pass" is a key phrase here. How accurately were God's words fulfilled?

___

B. Hezekiah's Sickness (2 Kings 20:1-11; 2 Chron. 32:24-26; Isa. 38:1-22)

Hezekiah's serious illness did not come after the events of chapter 19 but earlier, identified by 20:1 as "in those days." God's promise of 20:6, "I will deliver thee and this city out of the hand of the king of Assyria," points to a date sometime during Sennacherib's first invasion.
Does anything point to the fact that this sickness was in part a chastisement of Hezekiah by God?

___

List some important spiritual lessons to be learned from this story.

___

C. Captivity Pronounced (2 Kings 20:12-21; 2 Chron. 32:27-33; Isa. 39:1-8)

What would you consider to be the two most prominent items in this story?

___

What is the one main lesson taught?

What did Hezekiah mean by his words of verse 19?

II. COMMENTS

A. Sennacherib vs. Hezekiah (2 Kings 18:9–19:37; 2 Chron. 32:1-23; Isa. 36:1–39:8)

When Sennacherib came to fight against Jerusalem a second time, Hezekiah had no intentions of surrendering. Hezekiah was a man of faith and prayer, and he was also a worker. First, he cut off the water supply so that an invading army would not share its benefits. He closed the upper outlet of the waters of Gihon, directing them down to the west side of the city (2 Chron. 32:30) through a hand-made tunnel (2 Kings 20:20). Note: You may want to read about this famous tunnel and the Pool of Siloam in a Bible dictionary.) Then he made strong fortifications and weapons of defense (2 Chron. 32:5). But the strongest fortification was that which he made in the hearts of his people when he strengthened their faith in God by words of wisdom and courage that were backed up by his own example (2 Chron. 32:6-8).

B. Pronouncement of Captivity (2 Kings 20:12-21; 2 Chron. 32:27-33; Isa. 39:1-8)

It is sad to learn of any failure of a servant of God. David, a man after God's own heart, failed. In this part of the story we read that Hezekiah, a second David in his attitude of heart toward God, was lifted up with pride. He was proud of the honors that God had put upon him, proud of the success and victories that God had given him, proud of the honors shown him by other nations, and proud of his riches and possessions (2 Chron. 32:22-30).

And now a further honor was shown him. The king of Babylon, that great eastern power that was soon to overcome even Assyria, sent messengers with letters and a present to congratulate Hezekiah on his recovery and "to inquire of the wonder that was done in the land." This "wonder" may have been the miraculous destruction of the Assyrian army, or the return of the shadow on the dial of Ahaz (2 Chron. 32:31).

Hezekiah had a great opportunity to testify to a pagan monarch of the mighty power and grace of his God. But so far as the

93

record states he said not one word about God, about God's answers to his prayers, or of the mighty miracles and deliverances. Instead he directed the tour of his kingdom in a way that exalted himself. He may possibly have had in mind impressing the Babylonians to enter into an alliance with him against Assyria.

This failure on Hezekiah's part brought a sharp rebuke from Isaiah and a prophecy of the captivity of all Judah by the Babylonians (2 Kings 20:14-18). But how blessed it is to read that Hezekiah, like David, when his attention was called to his sin, humbled himself and bowed to the will of God (2 Kings 20:19; 2 Chron. 32:24-26; Isa. 39:8). He had learned through a lifetime of fellowship with God that God's word—whether it brings rest or judgment—is always good. As an afterthought, and not in a selfish spirit, Hezekiah expressed gratefulness to God that he would not live to see the captivity of his people. "Is it not so, if there is peace and security in my time?" (2 Kings 20:19, Berkeley. Cf. 2 Chron. 32:26. Note especially a similar reference in 2 Kings 22:20.)

III. SUMMARY

That the kingdom of Judah outlived the northern kingdom of Israel was due in large part to the leadership of the kings. Most of Judah's long-reigning kings were righteous, whereas all of Israel's kings were evil. It was fortunate for Judah that at the time of Israel's fall Judah was ruled by such a good king as Hezekiah, whom God used to purge the corruptions of his father, Ahaz, and restore true worship to the kingdom. How enduring were the fruits of Hezekiah's reign will be learned in the next and final lesson of this manual.

Lesson 11

Last Years of Judah

The prophetic decree of Judah's fall had already been spoken, so the fact of coming judgment was sure. But the ensuing years of the nation's history would reveal to what degree of intensity God's judgment would fall, and who would constitute the believing remnant.

The fall of Jerusalem took place one hundred years after Hezekiah's death. During that time Judah had seven kings. Study the *Charts of Kings and Prophets* (pp. 110-11) and observe that of the seven kings, two served relatively long; and of the two, one was evil (Manasseh) and one was good (Josiah). Observe also from the chart that many prophets of God ministered to Judah during the last fifty years, of whom Jeremiah was the chief.

Because of limitation of space in this manual, we are compressing the remainder of Kings and Chronicles into one lesson. If you wish to study this lesson in two parts, the following breakdown is suggested:

Manasseh, Amon, and Josiah	Last Four Kings, and Fall of Jerusalem
2 Kings 21:1—23:30	2 Kings 23:31—25:30
2 Chronicles 33:1—35:27	2 Chronicles 36:1-23

I. ANALYSIS

Our study of the last chapters of Kings and Chronicles will be centered on two subjects: (1) the last kings of Judah and (2) the fall of Jerusalem.

95

A. The Last Kings of Judah

In studying each of these kings, first read the Bible passages, then record observations of such important items as:

1. key events and deeds
2. the king's heart, and the people's heart
3. relations to foreign nations
4. ministries of prophets
5. words of God, and responses of the people

Follow the further suggestions for study given under each king cited, recording your observations whenever possible.

1. *Manasseh* (2 Kings 21:1-18; 2 Chron. 33:1-20)
Manasseh reigned the longest of all the Hebrew kings. Note by the *Chart of Kings and Prophets* that he was co-regent with Hezekiah for a few years.
How is Manasseh compared with other kings of Judah and Israel?

_____

_____

How is Manasseh compared with rulers of foreign nations?

_____

List some of the major sins committed by Manasseh.

_____

_____

Note Manasseh's conversion as recorded in 2 Chronicles. This took place toward the end of his reign. From the description given, how genuine was his conversion?

_____

_____

Why do you suppose this vital experience was not recorded in Kings?

_____

What lessons may be learned from Manasseh's life?

_____

2. *Amon* (2 Kings 21:19-26; 2 Chron. 33:21-25)
Observe that Amon followed Manasseh's *evil* ways, not the ways of

Manasseh's life after his conversion. Derive a spiritual lesson from this concerning influence.

_____

_____

3. *Josiah* (2 Kings 22:1–23:30; 2 Chron. 34:1–35:27)
The reign of Josiah was the last bright era of Judah's history. After you have read the passages, record some of your impressions.

_____

_____

Compare the description of Josiah's reign (2 Kings 22:2) with what was said about Hezekiah.

_____

Note that 2 Chronicles cites three important dates in the religious experience of Josiah's early life. Identify them:

1. 2 Chronicles 34:3

Age _____ Experience: _____

2. 2 Chronicles 34:3ff.

Age _____ Experience: _____

3. 2 Chronicles 34:8ff.

Age _____ Experience: _____

On a piece of paper record some of your observations on the highlights of Josiah's reform program, outlined as follows:
　　1. Repair of the Temple and discovery of the book of the law (2 Kings 22:3-20; 2 Chron. 34:8-28)
　　2. Reading of the law (2 Kings 23:1-2; 2 Chron. 34:29-30)
　　3. Renewal of the covenant (2 Kings 23:3; 2 Chron. 34:31-32)
　　4. Removal of idolatry (2 Kings 23:4-20; 2 Chron. 34:33-35)
(Read 1 Kings 13:1-2 in connection with 2 Kings 23:15-20. Notice the remarkable exactness of the prophecy and the matched exactness of the fulfillment.)

5. Restoration of the Passover observance (2 Kings 23:21-25; 2 Chron. 35:1-19)

* * *

How extensive, geographically, was Josiah's reform program? (Cf. 2 Kings 23:15; 2 Chron. 34:6-7, 21.)

_____

We learn from Jeremiah, who began his public ministry during Josiah's reign, that the participation of the people in this revival was more outward than inward. So after Josiah's death the people denied the Lord again. Read Jeremiah 11:1-13 for reference to this. What kind of worship does the Lord require?

_____

_____

_____

How is Josiah described in 2 Kings 23:25?

_____

Then what do the very next verses (26-27) say?

_____

What does this teach?

_____

Was there not some good fruit from the good reign of Josiah?

_____

_____

"It was loyalty to this same written word that provided the glimmer of hope for Judaism during the Exile [cf. Dan. 9:2], in its precarious restoration [Ezra 7:10; Mal. 4:6], and throughout the centuries down to the coming of Christ (Matt. 5:17-18)."[1]

4. *Jehoahaz* (2 Kings 23:31-34; 2 Chron. 36:1-4)
Who anointed Jehoahaz to be king? (2 Kings 23:30).

_____

Who then controlled the throne?

_____

1. Charles F. Pfeiffer and Everett F. Harrison, eds., *The Wycliffe Bible Commentary* (Chicago: Moody, 1962), p. 417.

Compare those days of Judah with those of centuries earlier when God's people were delivered from the bondage of Egypt. Recall some of the highlights of Judah's history in between.

5. *Jehoiakim* (2 Kings 23:34–24:7; 2 Chron. 36:4-8)
For further references to Jehoiakim's reign, read Jeremiah 22:13-15, 17; 26:21-24, 32:36. During this reign, Babylon won a decisive victory over Egypt in the battle of Carchemish, 605 B.C. This placed the land of Judah under control of the king of Babylon, Nebuchadnezzar (Nebuchadrezzar), who took captive Jehoiakim, a number of Jews, and some of the Temple vessels. It was at this time (605 B.C.) that the seventy-year captivity, prophesied by Jeremiah (Jer. 25:11; 20:10), began.

6. *Jehoiachin* (2 Kings 24:8-17; 2 Chron. 36:9-10)
Note in what a matter-of-fact way the conquests of the enemy are recorded. These were the days of the fulfillment of judgment.

7. *Zedekiah* (2 Kings 24:18-20; 2 Chron. 36:11-13)
Note that Chronicles makes clear that Zedekiah would not listen to Jeremiah and to Jeremiah's God. Refer to the book of Jeremiah for more information about Zedekiah (e.g., chaps. 32, 34, 37-39, 52).

B. The Fall of Jerusalem (2 Kings 25:1-30; 2 Chron. 36:14-21)

What was the immediate cause of Judah's fall and captivity? (2 Kings 24:20*b*)

_____

_____

What was the underlying cause? (2 Chron. 36:13*b*-16)

_____

_____

Observe from 2 Kings that Nebuchadnezzar let some people remain in Judah (2 Kings 25:22). What would be the reason for this?

_____

_____

_____

A Summary Question: As you think back over the events of the kingdoms of Israel and Judah, what things stand out as most prominent?

_____

_____

_____

_____

After you have thought about this for a while, list ten vital spiritual lessons that 2 Kings and 2 Chronicles teach the reader today.

_____

_____

_____

_____

_____

_____

_____

_____

_____

C. Epilogues (2 Kings 25:27-30; 2 Chron. 36:22-23)

The epilogues of the two books refer to two different events.

1. *Epilogue of 2 Kings*
The events of this paragraph are dated around 562 B.C. In what period (early, middle, latter) of the captivity was this?

_____

What kings are involved here?

_____

What ray of hope was beamed to the Jewish captives by this action of the captor?

_____

How does this paragraph serve as a concluding note for the book of 2 Kings?

_____

_____

2. *Epilogue of 2 Chronicles*
Compare this paragraph with the opening paragraph of Ezra. Ezra may have been the author of this continuous combined history of Chronicles and Ezra. The event of this paragraph is dated 538 B.C. Read Isaiah 44:28–45:5 to learn how Cyrus, king of Persia, was an instrument of God's providence concerning the remnant of His chosen people.

How does this paragraph relate to the message of Chronicles?

_____

_____

What is its significant teaching?

_____

_____

II. COMMENTS

A. Manasseh (2 Kings 21:1-18; 2 Chron. 33:1-20)

There is encouragement to every sinner in the fact that even such a man as Manasseh can be forgiven, restored, and used of God. Note that it was through affliction, fetters, and captivity that Manasseh was brought to repentance (2 Chron. 33:11-13). His captivity in Babylon cured Manasseh of idolatry, and from that time on to the end of his life he "knew that the Lord he was God."

Manasseh showed evidence of true repentance after his conversion. During the last years of his life he seems to have earnestly tried to undo the wrong he had done (2 Chron. 33:14-16). But he found it impossible to fully turn back the tide that he had set in motion. He could not blot out all the effects of his early wickedness. However much one may repent of a sinful past, the *effect* of sin can never be wholly recalled. That is the saddest thing about sin. Let us take care how we trifle with it. It is the most fearful thing in the universe, and it carries its own retribution along with it.

B. Amon (2 Kings 21:19-26; 2 Chron. 33:21-25)

Amon's reign was evil like that of his father, Manasseh. His greater sin was that, unlike Manasseh, he refused to humble himself before the Lord. He hardened his heart, defied God, and died in rebellion against Him. His impenitence was his eternal ruin.

C. Josiah (2 Kings 22:1–23:30; 2 Chron. 34:1–35:27)

Josiah was the last of the "good" kings of Judah. He is often referred to as "the young reformer." His reform program was the last attempt to bring Judah back to the Lord before the end came.

The revival under Josiah was in many respects like that in the time of Hezekiah. Both began with the king. Both centered in the house of the Lord, were based upon the written Word of God, emphasized the Passover, and were followed by a cleansing of the land. And both secured God's presence and blessing, at least for a time.

Josiah did what he could to turn his nation to God, even as he himself had turned to God with all his heart. But the revival in Judah did not outlive the good king, and God's judgment fell (2 Kings 23:26-26). When Josiah died, Jeremiah was one of God's true children who mourned his departure.

D. Jehoahaz (2 Kings 23:31-34; 2 Chron. 36:1-4)

Josiah's involvement in international politics at the close of his career (2 Kings 23:29-30; 2 Chron. 35:20-25) not only brought death to Josiah but also put Judah under the heel of Egypt. The people of Judah chose Jehoahaz as their king, but they soon learned who their master was. Pharaoh-neco, king of Egypt, deposed Jehoahaz after he had served only three months, and made his brother Jehoiakim the king. The land was also taxed heavily by Egypt.

E. Jehoiakim (2 Kings 23:34–24:7; 2 Chron. 36:4-8)

Jehoiakim reestablished the idolatry that his father, Josiah, had abolished. He reigned in Jerusalem for eleven years, and for the first four years he paid a large tribute to Egypt by heavily taxing his people. Then in 605 B.C. the Babylonian king, Nebuchadnezzar, who had been gaining strength for some tears, defeated Neco at Carchemish, driving back the Egyptians to their own borders and taking control of the land of Judah. It was at this time that Nebuchadnezzar carried off to Babylon some of the Temple vessels and a group of Jewish captives. Daniel was one of those taken captive (cf. Dan. 1:1-3).

For three years Jehoiakim was subject to the king of Babylon. Then he rebelled with disastrous results. Marauding bands of the Chaldeans, Syrians, Moabites, and Ammonites, all under Babylon's rulership and probably led by officers of the king of Babylon, invaded Judah and laid it waste.

It is stated in 2 Kings 24:2-3 that the Lord sent these enemies against Judah in fulfillment of the prophecies He had made, because of their national sins (cf. 2 Kings 21:11-16).

F. Jehoiachin (2 Kings 24:8-17; 2 Chron. 36:9-10)

Jehoiachin was eighteen years old when he began to reign.[2] During his reign of three months, in the year 597 B.C., he was taken captive to Babylon along with ten thousand choice captives.

G. Zedekiah (2 Kings 24:18-20; 2 Chron. 36:11-13)

Zedekiah was the youngest son of the good king Josiah (cf. 2 Kings 24:17-18 with Jer. 37:1). He was the third son of Josiah to occupy the throne of Judah. His two elder brothers, Jehoahaz and Jehoiakim, were kings before him, as we have already studied.

None of these three sons of Josiah followed in their father's footsteps. Josiah had been a good man of tender heart, who heeded the voice of God and lived to please Him.

Zedekiah's heart was hard and stubborn and altogether evil. Not only did he do evil, but he refused to humble himself under the scrutiny of the Word of God. And as he rebelled against God, so did he rebel against Nebuchadnezzar, despite his oath (2 Chron. 36:13). Zedekiah was influential enough to cause the religious leaders and the people to follow him in wickedness and refuse to heed the voice of God (2 Chron. 36:14-16).

H. The Fall of Jerusalem (2 Kings 25:1-30; 2 Chron. 36:14-21)

The time of final judgment for the kingdom of Judah had arrived. God had waited and pleaded long and patiently with the people to turn to Him, but they would not. Deeper and deeper had they gone into sin, until king, priests, and people were utterly corrupt. And so the blow fell that demolished their city and their temple, destroyed their land, and took captive their people.

2. See *The Wycliffe Bible Commentary*, p. 420, on the "eight years" of 2 Chron. 36:9.

Had God's promises to David failed? Had God forgotten that in His covenant with David He had promised, "Thine house and thy kingdom shall be established for ever before thee: thy throne shall be established for ever" (2 Sam. 7:16)? By no means. Every promise of God is sure to be fulfilled, no matter how improbable or impossible that fulfillment may appear to men. Miraculously God preserved the line of David through the centuries following the captivity, and in the fullness of time His Son, the King of the Jews, was born, to sit on "the throne of his father David." Read Luke 1:31-33; Acts 2:29-32; 15:14-17 to see how believers in New Testament days saw Christ's reign as a fulfillment of God's promise to David.

We learn from 2 Chronicles 36:21 the reason for the seventy-year duration of Judah's captivity, as foretold by Jeremiah (Jer. 25:8-11). God's people had neglected the observing of seventy sabbatic years (or 490 years). (Read Lev. 25:1-5; 26:27-35.)

Although most of the inhabitants of Judah who had escaped death by the sword or famine were taken captive to Babylon, we learn that a few of the poorer people were left in the land (2 Kings 25:12). Over these the king of Babylon appointed Gedaliah as governor (2 Kings 24:22).

Gedaliah was a good man. He lived not in Jerusalem but in Mizpeh. When the captains of the army, who fled the night that Jerusalem surrendered after a three-year seige (2 Kings 25:1-4), heard that Gedaliah had been appointed governor, they came to him at Mizpeh and put themselves under his protection.

Jeremiah, at his own request, had been allowed to remain in Judea when the people of Judah were taken to Babylon. He and Gedaliah together would have been wise directors for the people who were left. (Read Jer. 40:1-12.) But the people forfeited a gracious opportunity, and before long they sought refuge in Egypt against Jeremiah's advice, with this judgment of God hanging over them: "As mine anger and my fury hath been poured forth upon you, when ye shall enter into Egypt: and ye shall be an execration, and an astonishment, and a curse, and a reproach; and ye shall see this place no more" (Jer. 42:1;8; read Jer. 40:13-43:7).

The epilogues of 2 Kings and 2 Chronicles are bright endings to dark stories.

Exactly in the *middle* of those seventy years of captivity—the midnight of their exile—favor was shown to their captive king, Jehoiachin (2 Kings 25:27-30). It was as though God would give them a sign to strengthen their faith in His promise of deliverance after the seventy years of captivity. So there was a ray of hope for them.

Second Chronicles closes in the same tone. The recorded action took place at the *end* of the seventy-year captivity. God had promised to restore the captives and rebuild Jerusalem at the end of seventy years, and Isaiah, two hundred years before Cyrus was born, had named him as the one through whom that should be accomplished (Isa. 44:24-28). Then the king of a foreign land was used of God to urge a return to the homeland and to the former ways of fellowship with God.

Conclusion

We have now finished our study of the crown period of Israel's history. In studying the many historical facts of the four books of Kings and Chronicles, we have had the blessed privilege of learning more about God and man. Are we better Christians for what we have learned?

God's people had insisted on being ruled by human kings, that they might be "like all nations" (1 Sam. 8:4-6). God granted their sinful demand, and the succeeding centuries were marred by innumerable tragic consequences.

Second Kings begins its story on a promising note, with the first seven chapters devoted to the ministry of two godly prophets, Elijah and Elisha. But the remedies that they prescribed for the healing of the people were refused, until the day came when "there was no remedy" (2 Chron. 36:16). God was merciful and long-suffering, but the day of judgment for grace rejected always finally arrives. Within the last nine chapters of 2 Kings are recorded the conquests of Israel and Judah by Assyria and Babylon, and the scattering of God's people throughout the lands of foreigners. There was no remedy, so there was death.

None of those kings, including the best of them, was able to bring about permanent peace. Who then can? Only the King of kings, Jesus Christ, of whom one hymn writer was inspired to write these familiar lines:

> Jesus shall reign where'er the sun
> Does his successive journeys run;
> His kingdom stretch from shore to shore,
> Till moons shall wax and wane no more.

Let ev'ry creature rise and bring
Peculiar honors to our King;
Angels descend with songs again,
And earth repeat the loud Amen!

ISAAC WATTS

KINGS OF ISRAEL

KINGS OF ISRAEL	YEARS* OF REIGN	CHARACTER	RELATIONS WITH JUDAH	DETHRONED BY	HISTORY
1 JEROBOAM	22	Bad	War		1 Kings 11:26—14:20 2 Chronicles 9:29—13:22
2 NADAB	2	Bad	War	Baasha	1 Kings 15:25-28
3 BAASHA	24	Bad	War		1 Kings 15:27—16:7 2 Chronicles 6:1-6
4 ELAH	2	Drunkard	War	Zimri	2 Kings 16:8-10
5 ZIMRI	7 days	Murderer	War	Omri	1 Kings 16:10-20
6 OMRI	12	Very Bad	War		1 Kings 16:16-27
7 AHAB	22	Exceedingly Wicked	Alliance		1 Kings 16:28—22:40 2 Chronicles 18:1-34
8 AHAZIAH	2	Bad	Peace		1 Kings 22:40, 51-53 2 Kings 1:1-17 2 Chronicles 20:35-37
9 JORAM	12	Bad	Alliance	Jehu	2 Kings 3:1-3; 9:14-25 2 Chronicles 22:5-7
10 JEHU	28	Bad	War		2 Kings 9:1—10:36 2 Chronicles 22:7-12
11 JEHOAHAZ	17	Bad	Peace		2 Kings 13:1-9
12 JEHOASH	16	Bad	War		2 King 13:10-25; 14:8-16 2 Chronicles 25:17-24
13 JEROBOAM II	41	Bad	Peace		2 Kings 14:23-29
14 ZECHARIAH	6 months	Bad	Peace	Shallum	2 Kings 15:8-12
15 SHALLUM	1 month	Bad	Peace	Menahem	2 Kings 15:13-15
16 MENAHEM	10	Bad	Peace		2 Kings 15:16-22
17 PEKAHIAH	2	Bad	Peace	Pekah	2 Kings 15:23-26
18 PEKAH	20	Bad	War	Hoshea	2 Kings 15:27-31 2 Chronicles 28:5-8
19 HOSHEA	9	Bad	Peace		2 Kings 17:1-41

* These figures, as recorded in the biblical text, do not always reflect coregencies of kings. (Same applies to the table on p. 109.) The "Chart of Kings and Prophets" (pp. 110-11) shows all the coregencies.

KINGS OF JUDAH

KINGS OF JUDAH	AGE BEGAN REIGNING	YEARS OF REIGN	CHARACTER	RELATIONS WITH ISRAEL	HISTORY
1 REHOBOAM	41	17	Bad	War	1 Kings 12:1—14:31 2 Chronicles 10:1—12:16
2 ABIJAM		3	Bad	War	1 Kings 15:1-8 2 Chronicles 13:1-22
3 ASA		41	Good	War	1 Kings 15:9-24 2 Chronicles 14:1—16:14
4 JEHOSHAPHAT	35	25	Good	Peace	1 Kings 22:41-50 2 Chronicles 17:1—20:37
5 JEHORAM	32	8	Bad	Peace	2 Kings 8:16-24 2 Chronicles 21:1-20
6 AHAZIAH	22	1	Bad	Alliance	2 Kings 8:25-29; 9:27-29 2 Chronicles 22:1-9
7 ATHALIAH (queen)		6	Bad	Peace	2 Kings 8:18, 25-28; 11:1-20 2 Chronicles 22:1—23:21; 24:7
8 JOASH	7	40	Good	Peace	2 Kings 11:1—12:21 2 Chronicles 22:10—24:27
9 AMAZIAH	25	29	Good	War	2 Kings 14:1-14 2 Chronicles 25:1-28
10 UZZIAH (Azariah)	16	52	Good	Peace	2 Kings 15:1-7 2 Chronicles 26:1-23
11 JOTHAM	25	16	Good	War	2 Kings 15:32-28 2 Chronicles 27:1-9
12 AHAZ	20	16	Bad	War	2 Kings 16:1-20 2 Chronicles 28:1-27
13 HEZEKIAH	25	29	Good		2 Kings 18:1—20:21 2 Chronicles 29:1—32:33
14 MANASSEH	12	55	Bad		2 Kings 21:1-18 2 Chronicles 33:1-20
15 AMON	22	2	Bad		2 Kings 21:19-23 2 Chronicles 33:21-25
16 JOSIAH	8	31	Good		2 Kings 22:1—23:30 2 Chronicles 34:1—35:27
17 JEHOAHAZ	23	3 months	Bad		2 Kings 23:31-33 2 Chronicles 36:1-4
18 JEHOIAKIM	25	11	Bad		2 Kings 23:34—24:5 2 Chronicles 36:5-7
19 JEHOIACHIN	18	3 months	Bad		2 Kings 24:6-16 2 Chronicles 36:8-10
20 ZEDEKIAH	21	11	Bad		2 Kings 24:17—25:7 2 Chronicles 36:11-21

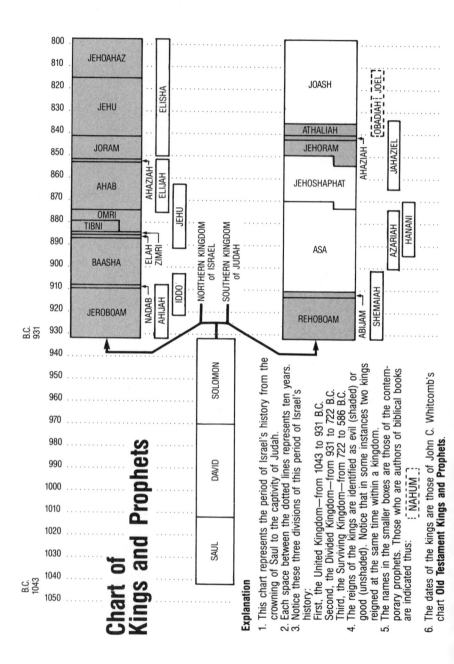

Chart of Kings and Prophets

Explanation

1. This chart represents the period of Israel's history from the crowning of Saul to the captivity of Judah.

2. Each space between the dotted lines represents ten years.

3. Notice these three divisions of this period of Israel's history:
   First, the United Kingdom—from 1043 to 931 B.C.
   Second, the Divided Kingdom—from 931 to 722 B.C.
   Third, the Surviving Kingdom—from 722 to 586 B.C.

4. The reigns of the kings are identified as evil (shaded) or good (unshaded). Notice that in some instances two kings reigned at the same time within a kingdom.

5. The names in the smaller boxes are those of the contemporary prophets. Those who are authors of biblical books are indicated thus: NAHUM

6. The dates of the kings are those of John C. Whitcomb's chart **Old Testament Kings and Prophets**.

110

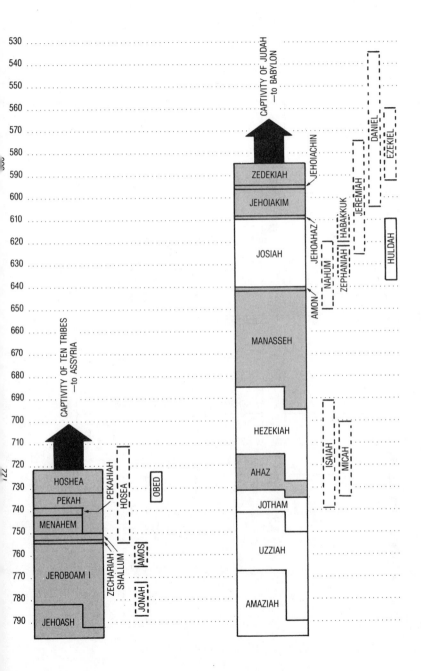

CAPTIVITY OF JUDAH
—to BABYLON

CAPTIVITY OF TEN TRIBES
—to ASSYRIA

530
540
550
560
570
580
590
600
610
620
630
640
650
660
670
680
690
700
710
720
730
740
750
760
770
780
790

ZEDEKIAH
JEHOIACHIN
JEHOIAKIM
JOSIAH
JEHOAHAZ
AMON
MANASSEH
HEZEKIAH
AHAZ
JOTHAM
UZZIAH
AMAZIAH

DANIEL
EZEKIEL
JEREMIAH
HABAKKUK
NAHUM
ZEPHANIAH
HULDAH
ISAIAH
MICAH

HOSHEA
PEKAH
PEKAHIAH
HOSEA
MENAHEM
ZECHARIAH
SHALLUM
OBED
AMOS
JEROBOAM I
JONAH
JEHOASH

111

THE SETTING OF KINGS AND CHRONICLES

FALL of SAMARIA

2 Kings 17

ISRAEL
NORTHERN KINGDOM —10 tribes—

JEROBOAM
12

AHAZIAH
ELIJAH — ELISHA
1

17

FIRST KINGS

SECOND KINGS

DAVID
SOLOMON

REHOBOAM

JEHOSHAPHAT

HEZEKIAH
MANASSEH
AMON
JOSIAH

25

25:27   EPILOGUE

1, 2 KINGS

1

1

12

UNITED KINGDOM
12 TRIBES

DIVIDED KINGDOM

SURVIVING KINGDOM

EXILE

JUDAH
SOUTHERN KINGDOM (BENJAMIN AND JUDAH)

SAUL   DAVID   SOLOMON

FIRST CHRONICLES

SECOND CHRONICLES

ADAM —→ (Genealogies)

Reign of David

Reign of Solomon

HISTORY of JUDAH to the CAPTIVITY

1

10

1

10

36

36

1, 2 CHRONICLES

B.C.
538
562
586

FALL of
JERUSALEM

2 Kings 25
2 Chronicles 36

722

931

971

1011

1043

DIVISION
of
KINGDOM

2 Kings 25
2 Chronicles 36

112

Bibliography

RESOURCES FOR FURTHER STUDY

Crockett, William Day. *A Harmony of the Books of Samuel, Kings and Chronicles*. Grand Rapids: Baker, 1954.

Free, J. P. *Archaeology and Bible History*. Wheaton: Van Kampen, 1950.

Jensen, Irving L. *Jensen's Survey of the Old Testament*. Chicago: Moody, 1978.

New International Version Study Bible. Grand Rapids: Zondervan, 1985.

The Ryrie Study Bible. Chicago: Moody, 1985.

Strong, James. *The Exhaustive Concordance of the Bible*. New York: Abingdon, 1890.

Tenney, Merrill C. *The Zondervan Pictorial Bible Dictionary*. Grand Rapids: Zondervan, 1963.

Unger, Merrill F. *The New Unger's Bible Handbook*. Chicago: Moody, 1984.

Young, Edward J. *An Introduction to the Old Testament*. Grand Rapids: Eerdmans, 1949.

COMMENTARIES AND TOPICAL STUDIES

Ellison, H. L. "I and II Kings" and "I and II Chronicles." In *The New Bible Commentary*, ed. F. Davidson. Grand Rapids: Eerdmans, 1953.

Farrar, Frederic W. *The Second Book of Kings*. New York: A. C. Armstrong, 1908.

Payne, J. Barton. "I and II Chronicles." In *The Wycliffe Bible Commentary*. Edited by Charles F. Pfeiffer and Everett F. Harrison. Chicago: Moody, 1962.

Pink, Arthur W. *Gleanings from Elisha*. Chicago: Moody, 1972.

Stigers, Harold, and John T. Gates. "First and Second Kings." In *The Wycliffe Bible Commentary*. Edited by Charles F. Pfeiffer and Everett F. Garrison. Chicago: Moody, 1962.

Zockler, Otto. *The Book of Chronicles*. Lange's Commentary. New York: Scribner, 1876.